Living
La Dolce Vita

Bring the
Passion, Laughter
and Serenity of Italy
into Your Daily Life

Raeleen D  r

 SOURCEBOOKS, INC.®
NAPERVILLE, ILLINOIS

Published by Sourcebooks, Inc.
P.O. Box 4410, Naperville, Illinois 60567-4410
(630) 961-3900
FAX: (630) 961-2168
www.sourcebooks.com

Library of Congress Cataloging-in-Publication Data

Mautner, Raeleen D'Agostino.
  Living la dolce vita : bring the passion, laughter and serenity of
Italy into your daily life / by Raeleen D'Agostino Mautner.
     p. cm.
  ISBN 1-57071-927-6 (Paperback : alk. paper)
  1. Italy—Civilization—20th century. 2. National characteristics,
Italian. 3. Italians—Social life and customs. 4. Social
values—Italy. I. Title.
DG451 .M326 2003
646.7—dc21
                                                                    2002153538
                                                                    2002153630

Printed and bound in the United States of America
BG   9   8   7   6   5   4

dedication

May this book honor the extraordinary Italian family that touched my life forever. Thank you, Giuseppe and Angelina D'Agostino; Domenico and Giuseppina Fodaro; and Marino and Rachele D'Agostino.

acknowledgments

I thank my family for their patience and for graciously respecting the long hours of solitude I needed in order to complete this book. A special note of gratitude also goes to my editor, Deb Werksman, whose expertise and suggestions have been invaluable in helping me to make this book all that it was meant to be. Finally, I would like to thank the president and publisher of Sourcebooks, Inc., Dominique Raccah, for believing in my idea in the first place, and in my ability to bring it to fruition.

table of contents

Preface	*vix*
Introduction	*xi*
Chapter One: The Power of Family	*1*
Chapter Two: The Art of Friendship	*27*
Chapter Three: The Unabashed Joy of Romance	*53*
Chapter Four: Meals that Nourish the Body and Soul	*79*
Chapter Five: Wealth that Goes Beyond Money	*101*
Chapter Six: Putting Your Best Foot Forward	*121*
Chapter Seven: Communicating With Words or Without	*141*
Chapter Eight: A Personal Spirituality	*163*
Chapter Nine: Attitude Is Everything	*183*
Conclusion	*197*
Epilogue: Finding the Wisdom of Your Own Cultural Heritage	*199*
References	*207*
Mediterranean Diet Pyramid	*219*
Further Reading	*221*
Index	*243*
About the Author	*247*

Raeleen D'Agostino and Sara, a very dear friend of mine, don't know each other. Yet Sara, without knowing it, has been a living example of the metamorphosis that the author of *Living La Dolce Vita* wishes for her readers.

Sara is the daughter of Italians who transferred to Long Island. Up until last year, she was a discontent eighteen-year-old—unsure of herself, shy, and lonely. She found consolation in eating chocolate and mountains of french fries, with the inevitable results of gaining excess weight. Diets and psychotherapy did not help.

As a last attempt, my friend decided to return to live in the *Castelli Romani* in Italy, where she was born and raised until the age of three. When I went to visit her this summer, I was speechless. Sara had transformed herself into a beautiful girl, and above all had returned to appreciating the joy of living.

The winning therapy was the self-immersion in the daily life of Montecompatri, a village outside of Rome where she now lives a life that is simple, healthy, stimulating, and rich in human interaction. She goes to the center of town each day to meet friends; she eats pasta and fresh garden vegetables seasoned with extra-virgin olive oil; she takes long walks in town, chatting and laughing with her companions; she has become interested in the arts, music, and politics. All of this has restored a joy in her that for a long time had been obscured.

Sara is a most eloquent example of the "therapy" that D'Agostino exhibits in this book, which is written with the competence acquired over years of research, the clarity that unmistakably belongs to a professor, and the Mediterranean passion that runs through her personality. In addition to a lively and tasty read, *Living La Dolce Vita* constitutes a precious vademecum for reclaiming our right—and duty—to be happy.

—*Dr. Tina Rella, Executive Director of Italian American Committee on Education, New York and Adjunct Professor of Italian at Nassau Community College, Garden City, New York*

There is a tense, dramatic quality, a shameless directness,
about the Italians, which is refreshing to foreigners accustomed
to Nordic self-control, to feigned or real frigidity.

—LUIGI BARZINI, ITALIAN JOURNALIST

No matter how many times I saw *The Wizard of Oz* as a kid, its magic
never staled. For that moment I was Dorothy, the wide-eyed, pigtailed
girl who desperately searched for an enchanted land called Oz. This
land would be breathtakingly adorned with deep red poppies and sun-
blazed fields of velvety green. While the wizard of this paradise turned
out to lack the power to go "poof" and blow trouble clouds out into
the horizon, what he did have was the wisdom and grace to show Oz's
visitors that all they ever needed was what they already had all along.
Archetypal wisdom—the wisdom of our collective humanity—is the
buried treasure of our souls. Its message easily gets lost in the daily bustle of life in a cutting-edge society, which at times spirals ahead of itself.
Fortunately, getting ahead of oneself is not an option in more traditional, time-weathered cultures, where the tempo still dawdles instead
of hastening by. It is in this stillness of observation that we remember
how to reconnect with our basic instinctual truths and experience lasting joy and well-being—which some of us liken to the promise of Oz.

No matter how many times I visit Italy, its magic never stales. I am breathless for the umpteenth time as my plane descends through the thick morning clouds to reveal the glorious emerald city below. My eyes, like Dorothy's, grow large with wonder and anticipation as we draw nearer the boot-shaped panorama, which is now a patchwork quilt of sunlit fields, and bodies of water so crystal blue they let you see through to their souls. I am always thirsty for her beauty, always hungry for her wisdom. The rest of America, too, seems to be fascinated and enchanted by, or at least curious about, Italy. When it comes to Italy, we are never quite satiated; we always want more. We want her leather, her gold, her art, her music, and her sensuality. But perhaps what we need most of all is her ability to relish life.

The signs are everywhere: Italy is definitely on our minds. Consider the recent five-fold increase in U.S. spending on Italian imports, the rising success of mafia-based television shows, and the skyrocketing record sales of tenors Bocelli and Pavarotti—in a culture where opera hasn't exactly been a common pleasure. Not surprisingly, a new Gallup poll reveals that America's favorite non-English-speaking country is, without a doubt, the *bel paese*, the beautiful country of Italy. Even the French are scurrying to be nicer to American tourists in hopes they will stop abandoning their country in favor of its boot-shaped competitor. America has always been sweet on Italy. She is not just a newfound chic of the *americani,* but, like an Italian marriage, our enamored attachment to this Old World paradise, while stable over the long-term, can fluctuate in intensity along the way.

Italy relishes the spotlight and is delighted by those who can appreciate her assets. She is proud of having preserved tradition while remaining cutting-edge among her modern-day competitors. She is not without her faults, but most of us are just as awed by her brilliance as we are intrigued by her shortcomings. Italian culture has overtly and covertly left its mark on the U.S.—from its very name (after Amerigo Vespucci), to its buildings, fashion, music, and cuisine. Italian towers, temples, cathedrals, and town squares have historically inspired American architects. Many of our top chefs are trained in the culinary sophistication of Parma, or the inspirational simplicity of Naples, where oil, basil, garlic, and tomatoes can be transformed into as many different dishes as there are days of the year. We now find ourselves eating pasta and pizza as matter-of-factly as we do hamburgers. Giotto, Raphael, Michelangelo, and Da Vinci have the ability to touch our souls even if we know nothing about art.

Cross-cultural psychologist Harry Triandis wrote that culture is society's memory of what has worked in the past. It is responsible for the assumptions people make about their environment, themselves, and the way people should act. It stands to reason that the older a culture is, the more refined these assumptions would be. This is analogous to the differences in reasoning skills between inexperienced youth and their wiser (in most cases) elderly counterparts. Italy, too, has "been around the block" a few times, and her cultural memory has been refined by experience. Her centuries-long history has been wrought with battle, starvation, plague, domination, and natural disaster. Consequently, it produced a people who learned not only how to survive unthinkable hardship, but also how to sing, paint, make love, and pray as if each day was a personal gift. The indestructible spirit that characterizes Italian life baffles observers. We long for a bit of this magic to rub off on ourselves. Americans may very well love Italy because in her we find a connection to all of mankind, and now, by learning the simple secrets of what makes the Italian *dolce vita* so *dolce*, sweet, we can bring the joy of Italy into our own homes and hearts.

The Purpose of This Book

This book will show you exactly how Italy's timeless culture inspires happiness in her people. Learning to hook into life's simple, under-stated joys assures a lasting state of personal well-being. You will gain a renewed, more focused appreciation for what you already have, and as you develop balance and serenity in your life, you will discover your own priorities for happiness. America's eternal quest for weight loss, super wealth, firmer skin, better relationships, smarter children, and more passionate love can be summed up in one word: happiness. We all want it. After all, our perception of happiness ultimately improves every other area of our life. When we feel joyful, we are not worried about jiggly thighs or under-eye circles or driving a car that is less expensive than that of our neighbor. While self-help books of all kinds fly off bookstore shelves each day, many of us still haven't found a way to smoothe away the harsh edges of life. For example, despite the astounding success of the diet and fitness sector, nearly three-fourths of us continue to suffer from illnesses related to excess weight and obesity. The U.S. also has the highest levels of childhood obesity, body image disturbances, and adolescent eating disorders in the world. More and more of us are dying of heart disease, despite the fact that much of heart disease is preventable with lifestyle modification.

The correlation between stress and physical health is also becoming increasingly evident. Many of us feel stressed and unhappy in our jobs or overwhelmed in our roles at home. As baby boomers are downsized in the workplace, they are simultaneously sandwiched between responsibilities to their own children and to aging or infirm parents. We no longer have the time to laugh or play, or to pursue the interests we used to love. Many of us don't have enough time to enjoy the money we work so hard to make. Others find most of their money is eaten up by credit card debt anyway. According to a recent survey, of the 76 percent of Americans who possess at least one credit card, 41 percent do not pay off the balance monthly and end up paying astronomical interest rates. This drains both wallet and peace of mind. Persistent unrelieved stress may eventually lead to physical and psychological ailments, such as depression and anxiety. Depression affects twice as many women as men and has been referred to as the common cold of mental disorders because it is so pervasive in our society. Anxiety-related disorders have also been steadily rising. The mobility of our society, which on one hand makes it technologically progressive, also leaves us feeling isolated and consumed with work. People turn to pills like Prozac, or alcohol, just to take the edge off a poorly balanced lifestyle.

This book shows you how to slow down your life and begin to live it with serenity and passion. Of course, Italians don't have all the answers for living the sweet life; nor does every Italian live by the wisdom of their own cultural heritage. But in general, when compared to the numbers in the U.S., the people of Italy's Mediterranean culture enjoy greater longevity, are less stressed, and show lower levels of heart disease, obesity, and general mental disturbance. It seems that a lifestyle based on the Mediterranean diet, combined with plenty of physical activity and social interaction, and a mentality disposed to "rolling with the punches" makes for a strong mind, body, and soul. These simple elements of well-being can be Italy's greatest legacy to us.

Italy's culture spans thousands of years: it is one of the oldest civilized countries on the planet. Besides the cultural influence of the ancient Greeks, Romans, and Etruscans, the Roman Empire established the principles of law by which we still live today. Testimony to the sophisticated genius of the early Italian people lies in their engineering, architectural structures, roads, and irrigation systems. There is also evidence of early appreciation for the arts, love, and music in everyday life. The early Romans already had the knack for striking a balance between intellectual pursuits, productivity, and enjoyment of life. This is all very important in understanding what makes the Italian culture revolutionary, yet in many ways unchanging. Throughout the centuries, Italy has weathered the hardships of foreign occupation, national disaster, starvation, domination, the destruction of war, and, more recently, terrorism. The cultural elements responsible for her people's survival gradually became the stable, immutable keys to their well-being. Experiential wisdom and ingenuity gave the Italians the ability to survive, adapt, and live serenely no matter what life has in store. Theirs is a complex culture whose lifestyle is nevertheless surprisingly straightforward and based on several powerful principles, which, coincidentally, also correlate with modern psychological findings on happiness. My goal is not only to inform and entertain you, but also to give you specific ideas on how you too can incorporate these *dolce vita* practices into your own life.

The first principle deals with keeping **family** ties strong. A historical distrust of politics, law, and authority in general make the family unit the main social structure in Italy. It is the seat of warmth, love, and security, giving each member a sense of belonging and importance. Italians maintain strong, lasting ties with grandparents, aunts and uncles, and cousins. If you are connected to family, or those you consider to be like family, you will never feel lonely.

After family, the second principle focuses on the importance of **friendship.** Italians say *chi trova un amico trova un tesoro*, he who finds a friend has found a treasure. Friendship in Italy is serious business; cultivating two or three solid friendships is preferable to maintaining numerous superficial relationships. A friend is willing to do a favor at any time and any place, and the small irritations of closeness are overlooked. Not making time for friends is inconceivable. Neither physical nor emotional distance has a place in true friendship. A real friend tells you what you need to know, and that is something to be grateful for, not offended by.

Third is the principle of **love** and romance. In a land where half-naked bodies adorn billboards to push dish detergent, you can be sure that Italy is not love-shy. The message of passion is everywhere—in art, writing, and music. There is nothing more emotional than a Neapolitan love ballad, or more sensual than a breathtaking Renaissance sculpture. Love is both unabashed and elevated to near-sanctity, and forgiveness and the willingness to try again makes most marriages indestructible.

You won't be surprised when I tell you that the fourth principle involves **the mealtime experience**. The central source of psychological and physical nourishment in every Italian home is, without a doubt, the family dinner table. It is where simple nutritious food makes the body strong and warmth and love fortify the soul. Mediterranean meals incorporate the simple fresh flavors of pasta, tomatoes, garlic, olive oil, fish, good crusty bread, cheese, and a healthy glass of table wine. When coupled with a dose of delicious company, mealtime becomes a true *dolce vita* phenomenon.

The fifth *bel paese* principle teaches us that the key to **wealth** must encompass more than money. Being "rich" means learning to get by with less and appreciate what you have. It means surrounding yourself with people you love. It means working to live—and not vice-versa. It means taking time to stop and admire the sun-topped peaks of *il Monte Rosa* in the springtime, or drink that afternoon *caffè*, coffee, at a local *bar*, coffeehouse, with a few friends. While it is important to save money and avoid debt, it is also important to know how to enjoy the countless other riches of life.

Sixth, **putting your best foot forward** is the rule of thumb in the sunny boot. Italians like to make a good impression through the clothes they wear, the cars they drive (clean and shiny, not necessarily new), and in the way they conduct themselves when out in public. Opportunities for physical fitness are built into the Italian lifestyle—people walk everywhere, or carouse around *in bici*, on a bicycle. It is not unusual to look out your window in the morning and see even elderly women in mink coats riding their bikes at a slow, steady pace with grocery bags either tucked into the wire baskets on the fronts of their bikes or wrapped around one of the handlebars!

Seventh is knowing how to **communicate** effectively, with words or without. Life is art, and Italians use their rich, colorful lexicon together with gestures and body language to get the message across, whether or not they use actual words. The human interchange is what is important, and when all is said and done, everyone understands each other quite well.

The eighth principle involves weaving a feeling of **spirituality** into the fabric of daily life. While the traditional Roman Catholic Church plays a less formal role in the lives of modern-day Italians, there continues to be a deep reverence for life and a sense of personal and social responsibility. Although they no longer attend church in droves, most Italians admit to communicating with God frequently; even on their way to work while riding their Vespas! A constant awareness of God's presence guides people's actions. This is reflected in how they see themselves and how they treat their neighbors.

The ninth and final principle pertains to the importance of having a positive **attitude**. Patience and civility are words that best characterize the Italian experience. This is most apparent in their ability to take life as it comes. Italy's daily bustle can be like an ocean in stormy weather: there are choppy whitecaps and occasional flooding, but it always manages to return to serenity, often through the comfort of maintaining daily routines. If they are used to going to a specific *bar* for coffee and pastry in the morning, they will likely frequent that same *bar* for years. Neither emotional outbursts, nor bureaucratic inefficiency, nor workplace issues, have the power to destroy the spirit. *Mi arrangio* is a common reaction to the frustrations of living in Italy.

It means, "I'll get by, no matter what," and many times a good *festa*, party, is just what is needed. Italians always find a reason to celebrate—be it a holy day, local produce fairs, or even one's name day. Partying is good, laughter is key, and regular R&R is an indispensable rejuvenator.

An author's inspiration is partially in the excitement of sharing what touches her personally. Writers want to believe they can make a valuable contribution to their readers. As an Italian-American author, researcher, psychology professor, and citizen of both the U.S. and Italy, my purpose in writing this book was twofold. First, I wanted to document and thereby preserve the specific aspects of Italian cultural attitudes that promote *benessere*, well-being. Second, I believe that sharing this information can help countless readers find serenity and rediscover joy in their lives.

This book is not meant to be ethnocentric, and I am not blind to Italy's faults. Certainly expatriates who thought life in Italy would guarantee them an instant fairly tale are promptly shocked by the reality of inefficient bureaucracy, mail that may or may not get delivered, and long lines at the town hall that often turn out to be the wrong lines anyway—although no one lets you know that until you reach the front. It can be maddening to have to empty out your wallet just to fill your tank with gasoline, or to not be able to resolve a utility bill because your records can't be retrieved from the heap on the floor. I realize that some Americans of Italian heritage may be hanging on to contrived fantasies of an Italy that doesn't exist now and maybe never did. Others are indeed aware of her faults, but love her nonetheless, as do native-born Italians themselves. In my opinion, objectivity about

Italy's defects is precisely what enables me to objectify her goodness—which is every bit as real and viable. From this goodness comes the intercultural approach to well-being that I offer you, my readers. This book is based on the strong points of a very old and wise culture—a culture that has had the chance to evolve and refine itself over thousands of years.

In writing about Italy's brand of well-being, I incorporated three important and essential elements: my own cross-cultural research (comparisons between Italian and U.S. cultures), the psychological findings on happiness and well-being, and my personal observations of growing up with an Italian family. My earliest training ground was the "old neighborhood," where the protagonists were not simply Italian immigrants, but also my grandparents, aunts and uncles, *paesani*, *comari*, *amici*, storekeepers, schoolteachers, librarians, bakers, bankers. I watched them closely. I listened and learned. Our family and community ties are what gave us a sense of purpose and belonging. In the neighborhood, we were not outsiders with funny ways, but dignified human beings who were deeply committed to one another, and that alone made us happy. Conversation was set in colorful blends of southern dialect: Neapolitan, Sicilian, Calabrese—it was all there. One set of my grandparents lived in our house, the other lived just a little way down the road. Over the years I came to realize how extraordinary these people were in their ability to adapt to a strange land where they were neither welcomed nor given help. They figured out how to start businesses despite the odds being stacked against them. Their mom-and-pop operations eventually flourished with a lot of elbow grease and tenacity, yet they always managed to savor the joy of planting personal gardens, making wine, and teaching all of us kids the thrill of dunking a fresh piece of Italian bread into a simmering pot of tomato sauce. Someone was always available to tell us stories about the "old country," even though we learned life's real lessons not so much through their words as through their example. While the stories and scenarios I use to illustrate my principles are based on real people, experiences, and observations, some details and all names have been changed in the interest of protecting privacy.

The stars of my old Italian neighborhood taught us how to survive hard times with our heads held high. They taught us about God, family and friends, simple nutrition, the dignity of hard work, the discipline to save money, and the importance of taking pride in oneself. Even today, despite the evolution of modern Italian society, these cultural tenets have endured both in Italy and in many Italian-American communities across the United States.

Psychological well-being, from a Freudian perspective, emphasizes the importance of love and work. Humanistic theories like those of Carl Rogers and Abraham Maslow focus on nurturing the positive side of human nature. Jungian psychology reminds us of the strong, lasting influence of our ancestral past. Cognitive behaviorism teaches us how to think rationally and help ourselves. Developmental theories underscore the importance of diet and exercise for maintaining well-being throughout the lifespan.

The Italian philosophy toward life reflects all of these core psychological principles. Italians will admit that life is what you make it and happiness is within everyone's reach. Ruminating in sad thoughts only keeps sadness alive. While it is important to enjoy life, it is also important to avoid excess and exaggeration. Whenever I spend time in Italy today, it is like stepping into a time machine that zooms me back to the principles I learned in childhood. I recall the importance of aesthetic beauty, good food, and plenty of social interaction. I remember that I should work hard but not at the expense of a well-rounded life. I am reminded to live simply and not complicate my life with things that don't matter. I am prodded to keep my body healthy, to acknowledge my soul, and to keep my interpersonal relationships strong and healthy too. While I am most grateful to my Italian grandparents for sharing their wisdom with me early on, it may have taken my psychological training—many years later—to confirm that everything they taught me was right on the money.

In a nutshell, the nine "Made in Italy" principles for living *la dolce vita* are:

1. Keep **family** ties alive and positive.
2. Make time for old **friends** and for making new ones.
3. Make **love** a part of everything you say and do in life.
4. Keep the **dinnertime** focus on good nutrition and good relationships.
5. Take care of your **money**, but remember what true wealth is.
6. Always put your **best foot forward** in all situations.
7. Improve your **communication** skills to improve your relationships.
8. Reconnect to **God** to gain meaning and appreciation for your life.
9. Cultivate a **positive attitude**; it will change your life.

Now it's time to take a little journey to Italy together and soak up some of the magic of the *bel paese* for ourselves. *Andiamo*, let's go!

chapter one

The Power of
Family

*Italy has often been defined, with only slight exaggeration, as noth-
ing more than a mosaic of millions of families, sticking together by
blind instinct, like colonies of insects.*

—LUIGI BARZINI, *THE ITALIANS*

In the Italian culture, loving relationships start at home. Family is the
focal point of Italian life, and Italy approaches family in much the
same way it approaches survival: with passion, perseverance, and
respect. Pope Pius XI once said, "The family is more sacred than the
state." To the Italian heart, even this is an understatement!

At times, keeping a family strong and psychologically healthy can be a
real challenge, but the reward is membership in a loving social network
that fosters well-being—and may even extend your life by preventing
loneliness. Research from the University of Chicago found that loneliness
undermines health in very specific ways. The report indicated that
changes in the family structure—a traditional source of emotional support—is partly responsible for loneliness and social isolation, which can
be health risk factors comparable to obesity and smoking. By the year
2010, there will be a 40 percent increase in the number of Americans
who live alone, according to U.S. Census projections. Of course, living
alone doesn't necessarily lead to loneliness or social isolation, just as living

with family in itself is no guarantee you will feel connected and loved. No matter what the configuration of your own family—be it a traditional family, a single-parent family, a stepfamily, a blended family, or a family of friends—there are effective *dolce vita* philosophies for enriching all core relationships and helping them to last over time. For instance, Italians have four basic rules about keeping the family unit solid:

1. Be realistic in your expectations about marriage.
2. Let forgiveness become second nature.
3. Be involved with your children's activities.
4. Make extended family your network of support.

Rule #1: Be realistic in your expectations about marriage.

Many Italians—and Americans—believe that the foundation of a strong family unit is a solid marriage. Yet, in the U.S., almost 50 percent of first marriages and 40 percent of all marriages end in divorce! As romantic as Italians are, they take a surprisingly realistic approach toward marriage and family. While long-term relationships are the goal—especially for the sake of the children—they realize that such partnerships do not come without a lot of tenacity and hard work. Avoiding unrealistic expectations about marriage from the start seems to help in avoiding breakups—and their negative effects on all family members—down the road. Healthy, realistic partnerships, in contrast, provide benefits to the entire family. People in good marriages generally tend to feel happier, take better care of themselves, have lower mortality rates, and experience more financial stability. Children also enjoy a greater sense of well-being when their parents have a happy marriage. However, when keeping the family together is not an option, it is important to know that divorced, remarried, and single parents have also been quite successful in creating positive family lives, especially if they recruit supportive extended-family members or close friends who are willing to offer stable, caring presences in their lives. No matter what your marital status is, in general, our *bel paese* brothers and sisters follow three important practices regarding marital expectations:

❦ Approach marriage with a practical mindset.
❦ Consider your familial network.
❦ Emphasize the values you and your partner share.

Approach marriage with a practical mindset.
An extreme example of this would be the arranged marriage of years ago. In my grandmother's time, for instance, arranged marriages—although not the romantic ideal—probably worked out because various family members participated in the selection of a mate to ensure a practical and functional match regarding finances, work, personality, and family background. Parents and extended family members helped prospective young couples avoid getting sidetracked. Looks and passion are fine, but the idea was, if you want to make a long-term relationship work, one must go beyond that. My grandmother came from a small Italian farming town in the late 1800s. Her cultural traditions didn't allow room for what we typically think of as "falling in love." Nevertheless, although her marriage was a union of practicality, it functioned well and grew into a loving relationship that benefited the entire family for more than fifty years.

While Italians do love passion, they don't let the thrill of romance blind them to practicality, or to the realities of their mate. Real love goes beyond looks and passion. It takes insight and maturity to recognize the seriousness of marital commitment and to be realistic about our expectations. Practical issues surrounding finances, personality, and in-law situations comprise very important areas of give-and-take. A willingness to work together, as my grandparents did, fosters a collaborative spirit of mutual respect, which only strengthens the bonds of love.

Consider your familial network.
In Italy, extended family opinion and contribution count big when it comes to family matters. Couples of all ages involve their parents, in-laws, and other extended family in their activities and frequently seek their advice and support. Often grandparents on both sides love to watch the kids, which makes things easier for the couple to work on other projects together, or simply to go out for a nice, quiet dinner. Whether you are married, widowed, or single, look around you and take stock of your resources. Think about current or former family members and in-laws who would love to be counted in as part of your support network. Contact them. Count on the support of those who care about you and will look out for your best interests. Often their support can make it easier for your relationship to succeed. Don't make enemies of in-laws if you can avoid it. Know how to relate to them in a way that is open and assertive—and not aggressive nor passive.

If you feel you can use some wisdom, why not turn to the family elders? My *nonna napolitana,* Neapolitan grandmother, shared her views about marriage whenever I needed advice. I consider myself more than lucky to have had her wisdom so readily available to me. She by no means had an easy or ordinary life, but her green eyes would twinkle when I approached her for counsel:

"Your grandfather and I made the best of whatever we were faced with. That was the key in getting along. We worked together and didn't have time to spend fighting over the silly things. There was too much to do in a day. He was a good man. He was a good provider, a good father, and a good companion. *Gli volevo assai bene,* I cared for him very much." I knew she wasn't talking about the kind of knock-your-socks-off love you see on soap operas. She was referring to something much more sturdy and perhaps even something more profound.

Emphasize the values you and your partner share.
If you stop and make a list of what your closest friends have in common, you will find that they are probably similar to you in background, interest, attitudes, and beliefs. The field of social psychology tells us that similarity—at least in the important values—is indeed one of the main factors in interpersonal attraction. As it turns out, it works the same way when choosing a mate. Research shows that personality traits and values are closely matched in couples who have long-term happy marriages. When choosing a partner, we generally look for traits such as kindness, understanding, adaptability, and intelligence. It doesn't matter if we differ on the superficial things—what does matter is that our general philosophies match up on major issues that are important to us both, such as family finances or how we want to raise our children. A friend of mine from Perugia recently reminded me of a very old saying among

Italians that is still used frequently today: *Mogli (mariti) e buoi de'* *paesi tuoi,* Choose oxen and wives (or husbands) from your own hometown. Of course, this is not to be taken literally, but you get the idea! An important variation on this theme is to remember what those shared values are, and continue to talk about them and find ways to keep them alive throughout the life of the relationship. This will help you to renew your commitment to each other and remember what brought you together in the first place.

Rule #2: Let forgiveness become second nature.

I am sure you have heard it said that when you forgive someone who has hurt you, you are not doing it for them, but for yourself. We all know how stressed and drained we feel when we get angry with members of our family. Well, stress is one thing, but pent-up anger does more than wreak havoc with our emotions. According to research in the field of psychoneuroimmunology—a specialty that focuses on the connection between body and brain—stress, upsetting thoughts, and negative emotions can actually weaken our immune systems and make us more susceptible to disease! Italians live with an implicit presumption of human imperfection. I always marvel at how hard it is to seriously irritate my Italian colleagues and friends. The main reason is their forgiving lifestyle. Three principle *dolce vita* practices regarding forgiveness are as follows:

❦ Don't take mere differences of opinion personally.
❦ Don't waste energy fighting over things you can just as easily overlook.
❦ Don't hold long-term grudges—not even for serious offenses.

Don't take differences of opinion personally.

Here is a surefire way to deepen your family's sense of unity: let everyone feel they can express their own viewpoint without fear they will be condemned or ridiculed. Italians like to express their opinions with emotion and gusto, yet at other times I've witnessed Italian arguments that were artfully restrained expositions of logic. No matter what your style of self-expression, make it a rule in your family that all opinions count. Think about it: how can you ever learn anything new if yours is the only opinion you know? Whether or not you agree with your sister, brother, mother, or father-in-law, listening patiently and carefully to their side of the story not only says, "You're important to me"; it also strengthens your bonds of closeness and mutual respect.

Don't waste energy fighting over the small things.

There is nothing that kills family serenity faster than belaboring insignificant disagreements. The Italian attitude toward child discipline exemplifies the value of letting small things go in the name of family harmony.

With the population growth rate as low as it is in Italy today, it seems like kids are on the brink of becoming an extinct species. As a result, to an outside observer it might seem that Italian children can get away with anything. Interestingly, you will rarely observe outright spoiled behavior in these kids. Why? Because Italians use discipline wisely and sparingly, and mainly only for offenses that count toward character. When I was growing up, my sister and I would be mildly reprimanded and then sent to our rooms for a couple of hours if we were caught in a hair-tugging fight. It was a whole different ballgame if we were caught lying, and the punishment increased exponentially.

Why? Because our parents knew we would eventually figure out on our own that hair-pulling would get us nowhere, but they were not about to let dishonesty become part of our character as adults!

Once when I was in Rome, I stopped to visit my cousin Maria, who had just given birth to her second child. As we sat around the table to enjoy a nice cup of espresso, two-year old Oreste began running wild around the room, spinning and jumping and squealing at the top of his lungs. While it was annoying to me to try and keep a conversation going with his mother, my cousin just continued to smile calmly and nurse her newborn. "I love your beautiful singing voice!" she exclaimed happily to her whirlwind son. Then, turning to me, she added with a smile, "Oreste doesn't quite know what to make of his baby sister yet."

I thought to myself, "This woman has the patience of a saint." Yet less than ten minutes later her face and vocal intonation grew stern, causing Oreste's whole demeanor to change accordingly. What made the difference? This time she reprimanded him sharply—for a character offense. I had taken a little toy out of my purse which I had brought for Ore' from America. He reacted the way any other child of that age might have; he grabbed it from my hand and started to play with it—without saying "thank you"!

Don't hold long-term grudges.

Has a family member ever hurt your feelings so badly that you stopped talking to them for years? It sounds extreme, but I'm sure many of you have had just such a situation and know what I'm talking about. If only we adults had our kids' natural ability to wipe the emotional slate clean after we get angry!

Luigi Barzini once remarked that everyone has a small corner deep down inside of us that is Italian. It is that part "which finds regimentation irksome, the dangers of war frightening, and strict morality stifling." This thought is a fitting metaphor for the way Italians generally handle family arguments:

❦ First, acknowledging that human beings do have emotion, the goal isn't to make ourselves feel nothing or become flat and lifeless in order to get along. We all feel stifled by the thought of a life of flat regimentation.

❦ Second, we must remember that differences of opinion within families can sometimes lead to emotional overkill.

❦ Finally, just as Italians have learned to fear the implications of war over the centuries, they have also learned to think twice about letting quarrels turn into broken family relationships. In other words, we must pick and choose our battles very carefully.

Unfortunately, sometimes our anger gets the better of us, and holding a grudge seems like the easiest way out. It is actually the coward's way out. It is easier if we don't have to deal with that person. At the same time, holding a grudge is the same as holding on to your anger—an emotion that only hurts you. The good news is that there is a simple way to break a cycle of anger and negativity. Psychologists such as Donald Meichenbaum believe that anger between family members can be diffused if you look at anger as a problem to be solved. It helps to take a pencil and paper and write it all out. Write a statement of the problem, make a list of things you can do about it, and then take action and try your ideas out. You will be amazed at how positively the other person usually responds when you take the initiative to reach out and end a family rift. After all, if family is where we first learn the important lessons of life, it should also be where forgiveness starts. If you think about it, the idea of staying angry with someone for years sounds pretty absurd in light of the life-threatening situations that people are faced with every day, all over the world. Let's take a stance and make forgiveness win out over anger!

Rule #3: Be involved with your children's activities.

A wise *dolce vita* practice for maintaining close-knit families is to participate actively in the lives of your children. According to parenting experts, one of the basic ingredients for fostering a positive parent-child relationship is making sure you spend at least some enjoyable time together each day. My friends Cinzia and Ugo are never home on the weekends. Both their eleven-year-old son and seventeen-year-old daughter are soccer players for youth teams in Rome. Ugo is the first aid assistant to the coach of his son's team, and Cinzia writes up the results of both children's games for the local newspaper. Now that's involvement! The key is to do things that you all like doing. Ugo and Cinzia both love soccer. You might enjoy quiet time reading to your children, or going for nature walks along a local trail. Whatever it is, positive interactions make kids feel cared for and loved, and you're likely to see much less acting-out behavior in attempts to get your attention. Italian families will vacation together, spend weekends playing and shopping together, work on nightly homework together, and take walks together after supper. This closeness continues into adolescence and even beyond, since many grown Italian children in their late twenties and early thirties still live with their families.

There are many ways you can share meaningful time with your kids. When I turned on the television the other day, I saw a wonderful public announcement reminding us that we are our kids' best teachers. It showed a dad painting the inside of the garage alongside his little daughter to whom he had given a paintbrush, too. Then it showed a mom planting flowers with her young son and daughter. There are many more wonderful ways for parents and children to include each other in their respective lives: you can cook a meal together, rent a movie you can all watch, get haircuts together, or if your kids are old enough, you can even get a family membership to a gym. Remember that mutual involvement is the foundation for good feelings and strong relationships that won't disintegrate over time.

In Italy, in the past decade there has been a 50 percent increase of young adults living at home in the 25–29 year old range and a 60 percent increase among the 30–34 year old range.

Rule #4: Make extended family your network of support.

Most Italians enjoy the security of knowing they can pick up the phone at any time, or simply walk up a flight of stairs or a few yards down the road, and always be able to count on blood relatives. For instance, when my Sicilian friend's mother died five years ago, naturally she was devastated. Clementina's mother, like most Italian mothers and grandmothers, had always played an integral role in her life. She helped care for her grandchildren when they were small, and did thoughtful things all the time—like starting the supper when Clementina and her husband had to work late. Although the two families did not live under the same roof, they were close enough—just one backyard away—to be involved with each other on a daily basis over the years. Now that my friend's father was alone, she and her husband, without hesitation, made a simple modification to their own family routine to include her father for dinner each night. Also, instead of taking the camper to the shore on family vacations, as they had done every year, they began renting a small apartment in the same location so that her elderly father could join them on vacations without being uncomfortable.

Sangue, which literally means blood, is often used to allude to family, which is every bit as important to one's emotional health as real blood is to the health of the body. Unfortunately, you and I don't always have the luxury of living close to grandparents, aunts, uncles, and cousins, but there are surprisingly simple solutions to help you reintegrate all of those people into your life, no matter how long you have been out of touch. Remember that simply keeping in touch with "distant" relatives transforms them into close relatives, and the rewards are great in return for surprisingly little effort on your part. Here are some *dolce vita* practices for encouraging active extended-family interaction:

❦ Make the first phone call.
❦ Make technology (for example, the Internet) work for you.
❦ Combine family visits with activities you do anyway.

Make the first phone call.
The other day when I checked my phone messages I heard a vaguely familiar voice that really made my day. "Raeleen," the voice said, "I have thought about you so often I finally decided to pick up the phone and call you. I miss you! Call me when you get a chance. This is Cousin Anita." I was elated and called her back immediately to add my part to the apology for having lost touch. It makes most of us feel fantastic to get a simple phone call from a relative we haven't heard from in a while, just to let us know they were thinking of us. Remember that the next time you think of a cousin with whom you've lost touch, and pick up the phone immediately! It only takes a few seconds to make the first phone call, and in the process, you will brighten someone's day in addition to possibly rekindling a relation-

ship that can enrich both of your lives for years to come. Anita and I live only forty-five minutes apart, but as sometimes happens when you live life in the fast lane, we just weren't keeping in contact with each other. All it takes is that first phone call to reinitiate regular contact and then you can make plans to see each other, even if it's only once every month or two.

Make technology work for you.
With the way our society is now structured, many of us find ourselves living far away from loved ones—sometimes on opposite coasts! While modern technology can never replace human contact, it can do wonders to keep us feeling connected between visits. We use the Internet all the time to keep in touch with our friends and colleagues, but how about using a search engine to find the email addresses of long-lost relatives, or to supplement expensive long-distance phone calls you can't afford to make on a frequent basis? You can send pictures, or even create a family reunion "chat room" exclusively for you and your relatives. Although modern technology is partly responsible for our ever-changing family structure and distant geographical locations, it can also be the antidote for the very problem it has created. Why not put it to work to bring family back to the forefront?

Combine family visits with activities you do anyway.
The other day a friend and I were discussing family and she told me that her relatives live all the way on the West Coast, while of course she and her immediate family live on the East Coast. One of the ways they narrow the distance between each other is to combine family

vacations with relative reunions—what a brilliant idea! It takes a little imagination, but with a bit of investigation of what vacations spots and activities might be offered near your relatives' towns, you can have a family vacation that everyone will remember for years to come!

Earlier I mentioned that one way to build strong ties between children and parents is to participate in each other's activities. You start with something one of you does anyway, and let the other participate in some way. The same holds true for relatives, whether they are near or far away. Sometimes we don't have the time to meet Aunt Darcy for lunch in a restaurant. However, if you know that you and Aunt Darcy both read a lot, why not let her know when you're about to go book shopping and see if she wants to join you? Many bookstores now serve coffee; so if time permits, you can even discuss your books over a nice hot cappuccino.

There are other small ways that you can incorporate family "duty" with extended family pleasure. If your family looks forward to going out for pizza every Friday night, why not ask Cousin Lucy and her family if they'd like to go for pizza too? If you both go to the same dentist, why not plan your sixth-month check-ups for the same day and time? If you will be in the same town as one of your relatives for a business meeting, you might be able to squeeze in a quick lunch or supper. Be inventive, and you'll see how little it takes to refortify family bonds.

Some Additional Dolce Vita *Practices for Strong Family*
Maintain family traditions.
Passing tradition from one generation to another helps keep the soul of the family connected forever.

Thirty years ago, while visiting my family in Calabria, I met eighteen-year-old Gina and her younger brothers Luigi and Pino. They lived together with their parents, maternal grandparents, and a widowed aunt in a large but modest house on via Bartolo in the outskirts of Catanzarro. Calabria is at the bottom of the boot-shaped peninsula in the Mezzogiorno, the southern part of Italy. Gina's mother Lugia, the *signora della casa*, woman of the house, always made a fresh pot of chamomile tea or cappuccino for her pack in the mornings and placed fresh biscotti in a dish at the center of the table for dunking. Incidentally, if you are unfamiliar with the pleasure of *intingere*, dunking, then you don't know what you're missing! In Italy, everything gets dunked—peaches into wine, cookies into cappuccino, bread into tomato sauce—it's one of those magnificently simple pleasures that make life just a tad more enjoyable.

Today—thirty years later—Gina's house has changed very little. It has remained the "family house" for her and her husband. Some repairs were made to the crumbling stucco, and a new radio replaced the old one on the kitchen counter. Very little else has touched this time-resistant corner of the earth. Now Gina makes the chamomile tea or cappuccino, and her own kids do the dunking of biscotti. "What's this big deal about family values?" she remarked once when listening to the latest news with her sons on the U.S. political campaigns. "But what other values are there?"

Gina's brother Luigi still lives at home, running the family business since their father passed away. Pino took to the big time and made a name for himself as a banker in Milan. While he misses being around his sister and brother on a daily basis, he telephones and flies home for every major occasion. On those occasions, the maintenance of family tradition helps them to feel the continuity of past and future generations. It lends a concrete sense of closeness and belonging. Keeping up family tradition from generation to generation puts you in touch with your own personal history. It is also a gift that honors the rest of your family. If you don't think your family had any particular traditions—at holiday times or otherwise—do a little bit of research. Contact some older family members and ask them what traditions they grew up with. See if you can dust them off and give them a twist to make them your own. Similarly, you can invent your own family traditions that you pass on to your kids and theirs.

Your creativity and tenacity in making family an integral part of your life will reap unimaginable rewards toward your *benessere*, well-being.

Family as a source of self-esteem

When you treat the people in your family like VIPs, you will help them to feel better about who they are, and these positive results can last a life-

Interessante!

Mario Andretti, who is referred to as the greatest racecar driver of all time, came to this country in 1955 with his family of five and only $125 among them. A few days after arriving in America, Mario and his brother were given jobs in their uncle's garage in Nazareth, Pennsylvania. This extended family favor turned out to shape both boys' destinies. One day, a sprint car was towed into the garage, inspiring Mario, his brother Aldo, and some neighborhood friends to build their own racecar. The rest is history.

time. The effect is also reciprocal. How you relate to your spouse and children is how they will to relate to you. The field of psychology has many tenets and theories about the importance of family. Family is, after all, where you get your first sense of identity in infancy. The great humanistic psychologist Carl Rogers once wrote about "unconditional positive regard." This term means that all human beings need acceptance, respect, sympathy, warmth, and love—by virtue of simply being human. At the beginning of life, the first self-opinions we form are based on the information we get about ourselves from others. If we are lucky, our first experience of positive regard came from a mother who cooed and coddled us and made our every movement and sound seem like a gift from Heaven. Naturally, when your very first sense of who you are comes from a caregiver who cherishes you, it is easier to develop positive self-esteem of your own. However, many of us are not that lucky. Fortunately, it is never too late to start doling out positive regard by the bushel and making your kids—and yourself, too—feel like a million bucks. Make a concerted effort not to berate yourself constantly. Admit when you have made a mistake, but instead of beating yourself up for it, learn from it. Earned self-esteem is lasting self-esteem. Give yourself and your family members plenty of opportunities to succeed in daily life, then remember to appreciate all successes. Giving positive regard to your spouse and other family members will automatically cause a positive light to be reflected back to you, and you will feel the effects right away.

Tonight, when you are sitting around the dinner table, you can use this simple exercise. Try asking each other how your day went, and really listen and participate in the discussion. Show support. Show you are on their side. Don't be judgmental when someone is pouring his or her heart out to you. Instead, embrace them. Paraphrase what they say to make them feel you really understand them. Let your strong bond of *sangue* let everyone feel "we're in this life together and we will always be there for each other."

The family *casa*

Italians believe that the home is the backdrop of a family's life together. Make your surroundings as beautiful as you can. Whether you live in a modern condo or a sprawling Mediterranean villa, with a little effort you and your family can dream up fun projects to do together to give more warmth and serenity to your surroundings. In the traditional Italian family, one's house is an extension of the family's soul. It is to be kept simple and meticulously clean. It is treated like a member of the family. The Italian home is not to be traded, sold, or otherwise renovated, other than for routine repairs and needed restorations. It is not to be left alone, so as to avoid break-ins, even if the neighborhood hasn't had a break-in in the last millennium. My friend Nina still goes to her parents' house once a month to "watch" it while her mother and father go to their parish church meeting.

Brothers Gigi and Stefano have a fascinating house—a one-time historic villa—full of nooks and crannies, each with its own story to tell. The house, where they live with their elderly parents, sits on the periphery of Milan. The brothers run a technology-consulting studio in the basement, and *la casa*, the house, is the setting for their business and social lives. This particular property had been passed down for more generations than you and I could begin to conceive of. Many

Italian homes today are still in sense family heirlooms, which is why it is unthinkable to sell them. The home, for all of its good memories and bad, is a family's personal legacy.

My paternal grandparents' modest, yet cherished, house in our little Italian-American neighborhood was a two-family house, and every part of the house had a particular use. The upstairs was rented out for added income, the front of the house was turned into a little grocery storefront, the basement was a wine cellar and extra kitchen for canning and jarring and making sausages, and the backyard was a small-scale vineyard. As a little girl, I was enamored of the luscious smells of frying sausage and freshly pressed wine coming from inside my grandmother's house. I was also amazed by how spacious the house seemed to me. In reality, the rooms were quite small and they must have seemed even smaller when she was raising four children within their walls. But Angelina kept her house uncluttered, spotless, and organized, so the modest square footage seemed to go on to infinity. All spaces were treated with honor. There were family portraits on the wall, framed Italian frescoes on wood, and sitting on the bookcase was the old smash box accordion my father used to play as a kid. Everything about that house shared a little bit of family history with its visitors. When you entered, you immediately felt good.

If you want to make your house a feel-good haven too, sit down together as a family and decide on what would make it more fun and pleasurable for each of you. Would putting a new shade of paint on the kids' bedroom walls excite them? What about dusting off some of your old memorabilia and displaying them where all could enjoy? Would putting some fresh flowers on the fireplace mantle add cheer to the living room? What about deciding to eat in your dining room once a week just to make your family feel special? Maybe it's time to replace or repair the broken stereo so you can have more music in the background. Let each family member come up with their own ideas to make your house become an extension of your love for each other.

Let kids be kids

You might remember the story of my cousin Maria, who remained unflustered at having to nurse her new infant while her seemingly out-of-control toddler ran around like a whirling dervish. Maria is not the only Italian parent with a high tolerance for "unruly" behavior. In Italy, it is a common practice to let kids be kids. Kids like to run, they like to jump, and they like to scream once in a while to let off steam. In a society where we already come home from work a little stressed out, sometimes our patience is at ebb. Don't lose your temper! Go into the bathroom if you have to, and count to ten. Take a few deep breaths to calm yourself down. And remember that punishment, especially physical punishment, can have the opposite effect you are seeking. It is always good to talk to your child if you can, and set clear guidelines that are matched to their level of understanding. The thing to keep in mind is that children need space to explore, to create, and even to be testy in order to grow into the people they are supposed to become.

Psychologist David Elkind referred to the phenomenon of the "hurried child." Years ago, at least there were rites of passage that marked transition from one life stage to another. Now, with all but very few social markers gone, children in our society no longer get clear signals as to when certain behaviors are appropriate. They are often pressured to grow up faster than they are ready to. Clothing styles for young children have become increasingly provocative, which can present a danger in itself. Kids not only dress like mini-adults, but also try to act as if they have adult freedoms. They go to adult-theme movies, have sex at younger ages, and choose video games that turn bloodshed and killing into fun and games. Their thoughts and emotions are bombarded with a level of stimuli that even real adults have difficulty processing, but kids have no real framework to help put it into perspective. Emotionally, they are far from ready to be adults. Adolescents often feel pressured to go along with more than they are ready for, and in the worst case scenarios, end up feeling detached from family, running away from home, experimenting with drugs or prostitution, or joining gangs in search of approval and identity.

If you want to safeguard your kid's right to be a kid, offer them clear and reasonable behavioral guidelines without being either overly strict or overly permissive. Unless they go beyond those guidelines, let them have their fun and always let them know you adore them just for being who they are.

I laugh when I recall the reaction of one of my graduate students a week or two after I had lectured about child development and in particular about allowing a child to satisfy his curiosity by exploring the world around him. Maggie had such a proud look on her face in class. She raised her hand and said "This week, instead of getting mad at my son for writing on the white leather couches with crayon, I praised him for creating such a great picture!" Well, I think Maggie might have taken my point to the extreme!

Looking at marriage as "family"

We are all far from perfect, and sometimes make horrible, yet very human, mistakes. Many of us righteously think, "If my partner ever betrays me, we will be in divorce court within the week." Italians face marital human error in a much calmer way. Hasty decisions breed more error and more pain. What if your erring partner showed he was truly sorry and begged for your forgiveness? What if you were to think of your partner not just as a spouse, but also as "family," and thus every bit as important and "permanent" to the completeness of your life as are your parents or children? You might have the kind of reaction that my friends the DeNilos had when Pietro asked forgiveness for his own indiscretion. The couple remained together and decided to make their union stronger than ever. The reality is that the impact of family break-ups is nothing to be taken lightly. Italians try to preserve family cohesiveness at all costs, despite outside influences, and despite even the most unforgivable mistakes. While of course no one in Italy is condoning extramarital affairs (Italian men and women are both quite jealous), affairs don't necessarily signal the death of a marriage. While the decision to forgive is personal, and ultimately a gift you give to yourself, only you know if you can then go forward with your partner the way Pietro's wife decided to do.

"Our marriage," Susanna DeNilo told me, "like a lot of marriages in my country, was based on many factors, romantic love being only one. When Pietro and I married, we also married each other's mother, father, brothers, sisters, aunts, and uncles—which is essentially most of the people in the town! Why would you divorce a whole town? We chose to work things out."

It might be that the media's overemphasis on romantic love to the exclusion of the practical considerations of a relationship is partly responsible for high divorce rates. Many of us feel disappointed when the romance begins to fade, as it predictably does over time, and some psychologists say American society has fallen into a practice of "serial monogamy." That means we go through one marriage after another, ending the previous relationship when the frenzied passion dies. We don't have to let it come to that. We have options!

One of those options is giving each other another chance, because in doing so you are essentially giving the whole family another chance to stay together. If the offending party is truly remorseful, you can probably even build a better relationship from this point on. Divorce, like marriage, is a big commitment, and a lot of practical considerations should go into both. As Peter von Winter once said, "It is manlike (or womanlike) to punish, but godlike to forgive." Forgiving is not always easy, but Italians have an instinctive tendency to resist anything that threatens the unity of their families. If you deem your relationship worth saving, take advantage of outside resources such as counseling, church support groups, talking to trusted family members, or perhaps taking a marital sabbatical by getting away for a few days on your own to think about your priorities and the direction you want to take.

Family support
Despite changes in Italian family life over the last thirty years (including a birth rate of 1.19 births per woman, more women opting to work full time, more single parent homes, and greater use of techno-

Interessante!

While there is more decision-making equality between spouses today in Italy, some household roles remain traditional. The signora della casa, *for instance, is still the "heart" of the family. She arranges the family social calendar, interacts with her child's teachers at school, and is generally responsible for the family's public relations. Contrary to the old stereotype, the Italian mother of today keeps herself attractive and fashionable, and she is likely to be holding down a full-time job. She is not the short, stout lady in black that we see caricatured in TV commercials. The Italian government, incidentally, gives women generous maternity leave options to encourage family bonding right from the start.*

logical gadgets) the family has still managed to maintain its stability and most of its fundamental traditions, according to a recent summary of the Italian Censis.

One of the most important factors in keeping families stable in Italy is reciprocal reliance and mutual support. A recent cross-cultural survey found that Italian family members support each other mainly in the following ways:

❧ Help in the household
❧ Help in illness
❧ Financial help

* Help in the family
* Help with depression
* Advice

These might be some ways that you can offer (or ask for) help within your own family. Helping each other out will strengthen your solidarity as well as help you to appreciate each other even more than you already do.

Family *Festa*

As Nietzsche once put it, "Man alone suffers so excruciatingly in the world, that he was compelled to invent laughter." In other words, *lighten up!* When was the last time you had a party with as many relatives as you could round up? If it has been a while, why not just invent an occasion and start the planning now? When my mother died unexpectedly, one of the most important lessons I learned is that life is way too short, and often too fragile, to wait for the next "official" holiday to get together. In Italy, one finds a reason to celebrate anything and everything. Italy loves a celebration. Whether it is a marriage, a kid's communion, or a grandfather's birthday, what is most important is the effect that celebrations have on family love and solidarity. Togetherness is the real reason for celebration! Emotion is unabashedly expressed, as are physical displays of affection. What could be a more rejuvenating experience than the combination of good food, music, laughter, and family all around you? Now go, I think you have a party to plan!

chapter two

The Art of
Friendship

*In the face of a true friend a man sees as it were a second self. So
that where his friend is he is; if his friend be rich, he is not poor;
though he be weak, his friend's strength is his; and in his friend's
life he enjoys a second life after his own is finished.*

—MARCUS TULLIUS CICERO

From its northern Alpine border to the lush olive groves of southern
Sicily, practically every square kilometer of *lo stivale italiano,* the
Italian boot, gives testimony to its people's undeniable dedication to
amicizia, friendship. It is one of the constants of the culture that gives
the *dolce vita* its characteristic sweetness. A visitor will find the most
visible displays of friendship in the main *piazza,* the town square, of
every city, large or small. There, men, women, and children of every
age and description stroll down the avenue locking arms and exchanging animated dialogue in every conceivable dialect. But beyond the
chiacchiere, chatter, friendship takes on a profound and enduring
quality, which is fueled by genuine caring and altruism. Many Italians
describe friendship as the most important aspect of their life, equivalent to that of family. Intimate friends often *become* family, especially
when blood relatives are out of reach, or when familial relationships
are strained.

What is so important about having friends? A good friend makes you feel grounded, supported, respected, and cared for. They are our mirrors when we need to understand ourselves better. They are our teachers when we need to learn the important lessons of life. Friends are our playmates when we just want to let go and have fun, and they are our therapists when we're having trouble seeing things clearly. Why do we need friends? We need them to confirm or to challenge the ideas we express. We need their emotional support so we are not alone in celebrating our joys or grieving our sorrows. When the world seems to put you down, a close friend elevates you by making you feel important and cared for. Intimacy between friends can sometimes be stronger than that between even the closest of family members. There are many things we would reveal to a close friend that we wouldn't dream of telling most family members. There is also an increasing body of evidence from the fields of psychology and behavioral medicine that close relationships contribute to better physical and psychological well-being.

Italians honor friendship through their emotional and physical investment. There are five principal investments they make in order to be a friend and to have friends:

1. Spend the **time** it takes to cultivate new friends and maintain the old.
2. Go beyond the superficial to create **intimacy.**
3. Practice giving and receiving **affection.**
4. Be willing to **listen.**
5. Show **loyalty** in your words and actions.

Cultivate new friends and maintain the old.
How would you like to increase the number of friends you currently have and strengthen old friendships that you may have been neglecting? Let's start by clearing your calendar right now! Friendship, like anything else worth having—and keeping—takes time. Here are some time-oriented, *dolce vita* suggestions for making and keeping friends:

❧ Start by knowing what you want and what you are willing to give.
❧ Review the basics of social interaction.
❧ Select activities that you both enjoy.
❧ Schedule in "friend-time" as you would an appointment.
❧ Let your computer help—not hinder.
❧ Turn your commitment into a habit.

Start by knowing what you want and what you are willing to give.
As Socrates said, "Be slow to fall into friendship, but when thou art in, continue firm and constant." The process of making and keeping friends is not to be taken lightly, because it requires a strong commitment on your part. It is important to stop for a moment and think about out how friendship fits into the other dimensions of your life. How are the quality and quantity of your existing friendships? Is there anything you'd like to change?

Take a pencil and paper and start with a paragraph on what friendship means to you and what you want out of it. Do you want someone to hang out with on weekends? Someone who shares your career goals? Someone who shares your religious traditions and values? Someone who is in the same familial situation? Perhaps you'd like someone to talk to about everyday feelings, or you might like to befriend another couple who would enjoy going to the movies with you and your partner. Don't be ashamed to admit what you want from a relationship. It is human nature to weigh the costs against the rewards of any relationship that requires our commitment—it is called social exchange theory. Of course the other party, in deciding to commit to you, will be doing the same thing!

Next, figure out how much time per week you can devote to friendship. There should never be a week that goes by in which you have denied yourself time to socialize. Socializing helps put our lives into balance and makes us feel connected to humanity. You might decide you could dedicate Friday evenings and one evening during the week to looking for new friends or spending time with existing friends. Play around with it—you can always readjust and add or subtract time as you go along.

Finally, because friendship is a commitment of time, you should be as selective about the friends you decide to keep in your life as you are about choosing which new friends you want to include. Just as good relationships make a positive impact on your well-being, unhealthy relationships increase stress and leave us vulnerable to its consequences. Don't allow negative people to drain you of your time and your energy. Negativity is more contagious than the common cold, and it contaminates us even quicker. Weed your life of social toxins, just as you would rid your body of chemical toxins. Don't feel guilty about cutting ties with people who demean you, humiliate you, or harbor jealousy or ill will toward you or your loved ones. You don't have to be aggressive or offensive to get these people out of your life. Just be firm.

Review the basics of social interaction.
Deciding to make the time for friends doesn't automatically guarantee we will know how to enjoy ourselves in their company. Some of us have been working so hard, or studying so intensely, or sitting behind a computer for so long that we no longer feel at ease when making simple conversation. We are out of touch with the simple mechanics of *fare quattro chiacchiere con un amico*, which, loosely translated, means chewing the fat with a friend. Italians prefer it to aspirin for just about anything that ails you!

PierPaolo from Rome told me that on his way home from work every night, he stops at a certain coffee bar and spends about an hour and a half talking about politics; religion; *calcio*, soccer—just about anything. Then he goes home, eats dinner around eight, and spends the rest of the evening with his family.

"I don't think of it as a way to kill time," he explained. "Rather it is a way to make time come alive. Friends remind you of who you are even when you forget yourself. In my country, it is unthinkable not to make time to for friends."

PierPaolo's attitude illustrates that we don't need to engage in elaborate activities with friends; all we have to do is master (or re-master) the simple art of conversation. Talking face to face brings people closer than any other activity. Boning up on basic conversational skills is well worth the effort.

If you could use a quick brush-up lesson on the give-and-take of social interaction, here are four simple pointers to get you started:

1. Make the other person feel important and at ease when talking to you. Ask them about their interests without being invasive. Start with a common ground and let the dialogue roll! Have something to say! Be interesting. Listen to the news. Read books. Make sure, however, that you don't proselytize or come off as a "know-it-all."
2. Pick up on social cues. Social cues are the spoken and unspoken hints that tell you how the other person is receiving you. Back off if the other person seems to be distracted or uninterested when you talk. Change the conversation if you see it makes someone upset or depressed. Friendly conversation is a lot like a dance. You need to be synchronized with your partner in order for it to flow gracefully.
3. Give your new or old friend plenty of sincere appreciation. We can all use a pat on the back now and then to lift us up. Never give a compliment just to ingratiate yourself to the other person. It will always come across as insincere and maybe even offensive.

Select activities that you both enjoy.
When you are looking to spend time expanding your circle of friends, turn the activities that you normally love to do when you're alone into social events. If you like to garden, for example, how about going to a lecture on organic gardening at your local library, or joining the garden club in your hometown? When you are there, be the first one to initiate a conversation. It can be as simple as, "I love the difference in taste in organic string beans. What do you grow in your garden at home?" An open-ended question like this invites more than a simple "yes" or "no" response, and it is a clear invitation for a deeper

exchange. With old friends, concentrate on activities you both like to do. Scour the weekend newspaper to locate concerts, workshops, or group hikes; then pick up the phone and see if your friend(s) would like to join you.

Schedule "friend-time" as you would an appointment.
Finding the time to build close friendships works out perfectly in the Italian culture, where watches and clocks are dispensable and time is felt rather than announced. Intercultural experts confirm what visitors to Italy have long observed: the clock simply goes forward at a slower pace. The rhythm of life is calmly wound down. According to intercultural expert Alfons Trompenaar, Italy leans toward a past-present/synchronous orientation in its conceptualization of time. This means that Italians are likely to frame their current experiences in context with their past, reflecting an appreciation for their history, ancestors, and elders.

The synchronic nature of Italian culture explains the tendency to conduct activities simultaneously and with a less rigid concept of time. For Italians, time happens minute by minute. This allows for an unparalleled appreciation for life in the present moment, and may account for our observations about their characteristic zest for living. Without question, it is the richness of interpersonal relationships among the Italians that makes life in the *bel paese* meaningful.

So what do we do if we live in a culture whose time orientation, according to Trompenaar's classification, is future/sequential? Ours is undeniably a more future-oriented culture. We tend to do one task at a time and make lots of plans and timetables. Think of how many ways you organize and schedule your time right now. Do you keep a daily time calendar? Do you have a daily checklist of chores and check off one at a time? Have you recently sacrificed your free time in order to meet work deadlines? Do you sometimes postpone vacations, visits to friends and relatives, and recreational activities because you're too "swamped"?

While our dedication to advancement and hard work is admirable, it can also be a mixed blessing in terms of our social lives, and possibly our health. Although we can't change the culture we live in—nor do we necessarily want to—there is something we can to do to enjoy the best of both worlds. We, too, deserve to enjoy the *dolce vita* and can attain it within the parameters of our own culture. How? First, make a non-negotiable commitment to yourself to dedicate a percentage of your time to friendship. Second, use your current scheduling and organizational skills to help you keep this commitment by taking out that planner and blocking out weekly chunks of time for friendship. It's that simple!

Italian sociologist Francesco Alberoni says a friend is the "person that not only shows us the direction to take, but also travels part of the road with us." Psychological studies confirm that people who are stressed or anxious feel better when they share their feelings with friends who are going through similar experiences. You deserve to schedule time for you and your friends to accompany each other on the road of life.

Let your computer help—not hinder.
Italians are technology enthusiasts, and their use of the Internet has increased exponentially over the past few years. But I noticed this about the way Italians deal with their computers: they use it to sup-

plement—not substitute for—live interaction. Did you ever get so engrossed in an Internet search that you lost all track of time? Sometimes hours go by before you even notice. This would be an ideal chunk of time to dedicate to seeing friends in person. Italians are big on chat rooms, email, and Internet search engines, just like we are, but their tendency is to do most of their "surfing" late at night, before bed. The rest of the day is spent in live interaction with colleagues, friends, and family. This is especially true when the weather gets warm and people want to be out of their close quarters and into the open *piazze,* the town squares. With just a slight shifting around of your own schedule, you can do the same!

Here is the key to using the Internet to further your friendship goals: use the Internet to locate activities, to meet new friends online, and to spend some time in a chat room with friends who live far away. However, limit yourself to one to two hours either early in the morning or before bedtime so that excessive time in front of the PC won't interfere with getting out and enjoying people with whom you can make live eye contact.

Turn your commitment into a habit.

It takes about six to eight weeks to form a habit. Making a change in your life—whether adding a new behavior or cutting out an unhealthy one—requires that you allow for planning, slip-ups, and revision. Planning, of course, refers to the scheduling-in of time for friends. A slip-up means sliding back into your former harried lifestyle and neglecting to keep the time commitment you set aside for socializing. When this happens, it is time to revise your goals. Were you unrealistic in trying to set aside the amount of time you did originally? Make sure you're not just making excuses, though. For example, if you only set aside one evening a week for friends to begin with, don't try to cut that out, too; just juggle your schedule a little more and find a way to maintain your original commitment. If you really did set aside an unrealistic amount of time, revise so it will fit more easily into your lifestyle. Then you will be able to stick with it for the length of time it takes for behavior to be cemented into habit.

Go beyond the superficial to create intimacy.

Here are two things to remember if you want to turn acquaintances into close friends:

❦ Figure out what you are willing to offer.

❦ Be the first to offer, then keep in step with what the other person offers you.

Figure out what you are willing to offer.

This may sound distastefully practical, but if you don't plan where you want to go with your friendships ahead of time, you may end up scaring off the people you wish to get close to and attracting the ones that you don't! Determine how much of your time and energy you want to give to each friend or potential friend. How much of your personal feelings can you reveal without feeling like you have been inappropriate? For example, you might feel all right telling a new friend about something you flubbed at work, but not about having been abused as a child. Naturally, the closer the friendship, the more personal you can get. Thinking this through ahead of time will give you confidence in your interactions, and you won't end up feeling embarrassed or regretful afterward. While you should never have to talk about or do things you will later regret, inviting another person to get closer to you does involve some risk and vulnerability. If your efforts are rejected, don't take it personally.

Be the first to offer, then keep in step with what the other person offers you.
Be courageous and take the first step toward friendship. What have you got to lose? Sometimes we get so caught up in the daily *tran-tran,* routine, that we let the good stuff slide—like socializing. Dare to ask someone you don't know so well to go for a cup of coffee. Share a story about yourself. Most people will be delighted at the opportunity to reciprocate because they have been buried in their routines too! If you notice that the other person doesn't bite, or wants to keep the conversation on a superficial level, back off a little, and try again another time. It takes some people more time than others to build up trust. Give people space and trust your instincts as to when to move on.

Kahlil Gibran wrote in *The Prophet*, "And in the sweetness of friendship let there be laughter, and sharing of pleasures, for in the dew of little things the heart finds its morning and is refreshed." If this sharing is mutual and balanced, the friendship will feel right. If it is one-sided, then the side doing all the giving starts to wear out pretty quickly.

I ran into Signora Gamicchia at the grocery store several months ago. She is a relatively new Italian immigrant who loves America as much as any American-born citizen I have ever known, but she was having a little trouble getting used to the faster pace of our culture. She felt lonely and found herself longing to share laughter and conversation. "People here seem to get friendly with you right away, but then they go in their houses and you don't see them again! People close their doors when they get home, and they don't come back out. I miss going to neighbors' houses for a cup of coffee." Of course, I knew there was something the *signora* could do right away, and I took her to my house to tell her what it was, over a potently brewed double espresso.

"*Signora*," I said. "Just take the first step."

"Eh?"

"Ask your neighbors in for a cup of coffee, and see what happens."

Several weeks later I ran into the *signora* at church, where she ran up to me with a big smile. A couple of neighbors had declined her invitations to coffee, but there were three women who not only accepted, they even reciprocated with invitations of their own. The four of them are talking about starting a baking club and meeting regularly! That is social reciprocation at its best. All it took was for someone to reach out and take the first step.

When we get bogged down with the things we have to do, it is easy to brush off the "nonessential" dimensions of our lives, like socializing. Schools do the same thing when they drop courses like art, music, and physical education at the first sign of budget cuts. But sooner or later, everyone realizes that the "nonessential" courses are the most essential of all, for they are what give depth to the curriculum and inspire creativity. If you have fallen out of the friendship habit, get back into it by making the first step. If your effort goes unappreciated, don't take it personally—just try again with someone else. There are many people in the world who would love to have a friend exactly like you. These are relationships that will give your life dimension, richness, and meaning.

While I don't buy the notion that relationships should follow the "eye for an eye" principle, getting close to someone does require some kind of reciprocity when it comes to making contact with each other and exchanging self-revelations. There is such a thing as inappropriate disclosure, which in plain jargon means: Don't spill the whole jar of beans on the table at once. Did you ever know someone who told you her whole life story the first time you laid eyes on her? If you are like me, your first reaction might have been to head for the hills! Someone who reveals way more than you want to know without allowing time for a gradual, mutual intimacy shows a lack of sensitivity toward you, in addition to a lack of social skills in general—hardly a good prospect! On the other hand, it is equally frustrating to hit a wall of zipped lips when you're trying to get close to someone and they won't let you get beyond small talk. Communication between friends is like a dance that takes two, and the dance should even get better with the passage of time, *piano piano*...very slowly.

Practice giving and receiving affection.

There are three basic ways to show affection:

☙ Physical contact
☙ Verbal tenderness
☙ Thoughtful gestures

Physical contact

Your personal preference and the culture in which you live will determine the amount of physical contact you ultimately have with others. In a restaurant outside of Trapani, Sicily, I once counted the number of times two male friends touched each other as they ate lunch. In the first fifteen minutes alone, there were ten incidences of physical contact—some brief, others a bit longer. To Italians, touch is an indispensable tool when sharing confidences. Everyone walks everywhere *a braccetto,* arm in arm, whether they are two men, two women, or one of each. Although the goal isn't to change the entire culture we live in, we can reflect on how much physical touch we would like to have in our lives, keeping to the proxemics (unspoken rules of social distance) for our own culture. The need or desire for physical closeness varies with the individual. For example, James has still not recovered from the time he visited his wife's relatives in Italy, where cousin Pino insisted on interlocking arms and walking *a braccetto.* On the other hand, he is quite comfortable giving his male friends a quick hug, shaking their hands, or patting them on the back in the course of their conversation.

Communications expert Robert Bolton confirms that at certain times nonverbal responses are more appropriate than anything that might be spoken. Sometimes when the words won't come easily, a hug shared between friends says it all. You may, however, be a person who feels awkward about physical contact. It may conjure up connotations of evil, sexual malice, or harassment. That's OK. You should never do anything you feel is not right for you. Also, America's cultural norms are different than those in the more expressive, socially-oriented Italy. While we may not wish to lay our hands all over our friends when eating dinner in a restaurant, we can still take pleasure in scaled down versions of warm physical expressiveness. You decide on how much physical affection you want to give and receive. Are you comfortable touching and being touched by friends of the opposite sex? What kind of touch feels good to you (hugging, handholding, a quick caress on the head, etc)? Are there certain friends of the same gender that you feel more or less comfortable with in terms of mutual touch? Would you be OK with walking arm in arm with a friend, or simply giving a light touch on the shoulder once in a while to emphasize certain points in a conversation?

Physical gestures of affection can be a wonderful way to affirm your bond with close friends. All of us have an instinctual need for touch; newborn babies—even newborns in the animal kingdom—fail to thrive without the warmth of physical touch. Sometimes we get away from this important experience when we grow older. If you find yourself in need of human touch, start out by offering small affectionate gestures to your closest friends, if you aren't doing so already. See if they enjoy it, cringe, or return the gesture. Adding this kind of affection can bring friendship to new depths.

Verbal tenderness

Choose your words as carefully as you do your friends. Words are powerful tools that have a direct effect on how others react to you. I mentioned before that the only right way to give a compliment is to give a sincere one. Sincere compliments or words of appreciation can turn someone's whole day around. Once, when I was a teenager, I was asked by a recreation director to play my guitar for a group of elderly patients at a convalescent hospital. I played about an hour of the kind of music that I knew, but that I soon discovered was unknown to the patients. The more they requested particular songs, the more I had to deny their requests, and substitute them with tunes by Cream, The Doors, or the Rolling Stones. That night before going to bed, I thought about how dumb it was not to have figured out beforehand that I should have learned some more "classic" tunes for the occasion. However, about a week later, I received a thank-you note from the recreation director. She told me my selection of music was wonderful, and that lately she was hearing quite a few of the elderly patients humming Doors tunes! That note made me feel so good about myself that I kept it to this day, and still pull it out when I need a lift.

In addition to honest compliments, words of encouragement, support, and empathy go a long way for endearing yourself to a potential or existing friend. Telling someone you understand how they feel without giving advice, expressing your heartfelt condolences over a friend's difficulties, or making a quick phone call to congratulate a friend on a recent promotion are some important ways you can communicate verbal affection.

Thoughtful gestures

Thoughtful gestures make a person feel appreciated and cared for. There are so many little things you can do to make a friend feel good and let him know you are thinking of him. Think about sending a spontaneous email to ask how their day went or a card in the mail to remember their birthday. A small thank-you gift in return for a favor they recently did for you can be like a ray of unexpected sunshine in their day. My friend Marco, a research assistant at the University of Parma, enjoys dabbling in carpentry. A year ago, he made a special chair for the elderly parents of his longtime coworker Alberto, who is also his friend. He never asked to be paid, but every week to this day he gets a little "surprise" gift, delivered by Alberto on behalf of his folks. Sometimes this gift is a few fresh eggs that their chickens laid that morning; sometimes it is some homemade tortellini that the *signora* set aside for Marco when she made it for her family.

A thoughtful gesture not only brightens a person's day, it will also brighten your own when you see the smile on your friend's face, and it doesn't require a lot of time or money. Think of some special things you can do for your friends that don't require a lot of effort on your part, but that would mean a great deal to them. Can you baby-sit for your friend's toddler while she goes to the store? What about lending a book to a colleague who mentioned that he had an interest in a particular author? When you rake your own leaves, how about raking the leaves in your neighbor's front yard too? There are thousands of ways to let a person know you care.

Be willing to listen. Here are two dolce vita *practices that are guaranteed to build trust in your relationships:*

❦ When a friend talks to you, let them be the focal point of your **attention**.

❦ When asked for **advice**, give it honestly, but respectfully.

Attention

According to an Italian proverb, "From listening comes wisdom, and from speaking, repentance." Imagine you are having a frustrating day. You dial a friend's number and start to unload. After only one or two sentences your friend begins doling out unsolicited advice. You may not want advice. You may just want to *sfogarti,* vent a little. Your friend starts going into detail about her own experiences. Before you know it, it's not about you at all anymore—it's about her! Real empathic listening involves deeply hearing and reflecting on what the other person is saying and recognizing that their experience is unique. This is the kind of listening that makes the therapeutic relationship between a psychotherapist and client so effective, too. When a client knows he is truly being heard, he begins to heal. That is how powerful the gift of listening is! Sympathy means using your own frame of reference to understand someone else, but empathy requires putting yourself in that person's shoes and trying to understand them from their own point of view. According to humanist Carl Rogers, empathic listening is the greatest gift you can give a friend. The next time someone you care about needs to talk, give them your full attention, not your advice—unless asked.

Advice

This is the real moment of truth between friends. It is also where hearts become trusting, more so than in any other situation. You may have already learned this the hard way, but an important rule of thumb to keep in mind is: Don't give advice gratuitously, but if and when you are asked, give it honestly and respectfully. Most of the time we really don't want anyone to tell us we did something wrong, especially if we are already feeling that way. When we do ask for advice, what we are really asking for is support. That doesn't mean you have to lie. I have listened in on some shockingly honest advice doled out between friends in the *bel paese*. Typically, the more "unfiltered" advice is exchanged between close family members and very intimate lifelong friends, where there is total trust that the advice-giver has the person's best interests at heart. In all other situations, while the advice is still honest, there is a bit more care taken to not hurt the other person's feelings or dignity.

What do you say if a friend asks your advice about something that you feel they've messed up on? Simply tell them, "Okay, you might have goofed up, we all do, but *non abbatterti*," as the Italians say, don't get discouraged! In other words, always make your advice enabling and supportive. Help them think of positive solutions that will allow them to regain some peace of mind. Now that's camaraderie!

Show loyalty in your words and actions.

Loyalty, according to *The Merriam-Webster's Dictionary*, means faithfulness. When I asked my friend Roberta how she stays faithful to her most trusted friendships, she replied *"Si deve tollerare e perdonare,"* you have to be **tolerant** and **forgiving**.

When Arthur Helps said, "Tolerance is the only real test of civilization," he might have been referring to Italy. Tolerance and forgiveness characterize long-term Italian friendships. While you might see animated verbal disagreements as a matter of course among friends in Italy, you will also see the tenacity required to conclude all arguments on a favorable note and move on. Italians not only don't mind differences between people; they enjoy them. Besides, it takes too much energy to get bent out of shape over every argument. "As in marriage," Roberta said, "you have to let the little things go if you want a friend for life." We can all benefit by practicing tolerance and forgiveness.

Tolerance

While it is important to be honest with friends about what offends you, it is a mistake to think that you have to be verbal about every little thing that irritates you. Think of the last time that you were irritated about something a friend did or said. What was your reaction? How did you feel? You might have spoken out impulsively and regretted it later. Or you might have held your tongue and were glad you did because it all blew over quickly. Massimo, who is from Bari, in the Apulia region of Italy, once told me that intentionally hurting a friend with unkind words is like driving a nail into a piece of wood. "You can always remove the nail with an apology, but the impression of the nail remains even when the nail is pulled out of the wood." That is why it is so important to think before you speak!

An interesting and beneficial phenomenon occurs when you make a habit of practicing tolerance. As you learn to disregard unimportant irritations, you not only avoid hurting people you wish you hadn't, but you will also become less fragile emotionally as well as less impulsive. Little things will stop bothering you as much, and you will feel more confident in not having to respond to everything. Everyone wins!

Here is a simple way to acquire tolerance: the next time you feel yourself getting irritated with a friend, notice your physical warning signs and use them as a tool to help you stop and change directions before you react. What are your physical signs when irritated? Do your palms get sweaty? Does your face feel hot? Does your heart start to beat faster? These are all symptoms of the fight or flight response. They tell you your body is preparing for a stressful situation—like verbal retaliation! When you feel these symptoms, tell your friend to hold on a second with the excuse that you need to use the restroom. Go in the other room and do a quick assessment to determine if addressing this argument is really worth it, or will it possibly do more harm than good to the positive feelings between you? Remind yourself of how much this person means to you, and how many wonderful things they have done for you in the past. Keep in mind that your friend has probably let many small irritations slide, too.

Forgiveness

Since we visited the rationale for forgiveness in the chapter on family, I only need to include one additional thought. I previously said that forgiveness is a good thing for you to do. But I would also like you to consider it as good thing to ask for; especially when you believe you may have hurt someone through something you said or did. A heartfelt "I'm sorry" is rarely refused. Not only will asking pardon mean a great deal to a true friend, but it will also do wonders to make your friendship even better. Why? Whenever you take the emotional risk of asking forgiveness, it is a sign of trust and sincerity. Asking forgiveness is a visible, tangible testimony of how strong your commitment to this friendship is.

In addition to tolerance and forgiveness, here are a few simple ways to demonstrate loyalty in friendship. You will probably think of many more on your own!

❦ Never criticize your friend to other people.
❦ Defend your friend if others are saying unfair things about him or her.
❦ Be patient with friends. Always allow room for human error.
❦ Never end a conversation on an angry note.
❦ Be there for your friend when they are sick, grieving, or in need of help.

The story of Umberto and Rosario is a compelling portrait of loyalty between friends. Their friendship lasted for almost eighty years, starting in elementary school where they first learned to stand up for each other through thick and thin. As young men whose sole objective was to win ladies' hearts, the two once decided to get nose jobs on the spur of the moment. Together, they managed to pool their money and hopped a train to Milan, where they had read about a doctor who specialized in turning men into women-magnets. When they got older and Rosario was a little short on cash for an engagement ring, Umberto couldn't make a withdrawal from his account fast enough. They were godfathers to each other's children and eventually became partners in business, having decided they had both had enough of working for other people. Their families became close, their children grew up together, and even their grandchildren became friends.

When Umberto started to become forgetful and short-tempered, that didn't scare Rosario away. It also didn't scare Rosario away when Umberto failed to recognize him, or got so agitated that he threw a punch at his friend. When his Alzheimer's disease advanced to the point where he couldn't be left alone anymore, Rosario would go and sit with him so Umberto's wife could go out and run errands and keep her own doctor's appointments. Death was the only force strong enough to keep these two loyal friends apart, at least physically. Rosario, at 88, still refuses to say or remember one negative aspect about his beloved Umberto. In this way, the loyalty of their friendship lives on. As the Italian saying goes, *Chi trova un amico trova un tesoro*, he who finds a friend finds a treasure.

Some Additional Dolce Vita Practices for Extraordinary Friendships

Connect to each other's families.

Connectedness gives human beings a sense of security and belonging. In a traditional society, like Italy's, where people stay in the neighborhood they grew up in, it is likely that friends will know each other's families almost as well as they know their own. But while living in a more mobile society might make it harder for us to become familiar with each other's roots, there is nothing stopping us from becoming a treasured part of each other's families. Doing so gives you an additional "extended family" of your own!

Giancarlo and Vincenzo of Padova, for example, have been good friends for many years. They take family vacations together and celebrate each other's kids' birthdays as they would their own. Once, when Giancarlo asked Vincenzo and his wife to go for pizza, Vince replied, "I can't. Saturday I'm helping my *vecchietti*, elderly parents, press the grapes. They can't do it themselves anymore."

"Don't worry," Giancarlo assured him. "We'll have pizza another time. Maybe next week, OK?"

But that wasn't where it ended. That Saturday, when Vincenzo was in the *cantina*, the wine cellar of his parents' farmhouse, he heard a Vespa pull into the driveway.

Giancarlo greeted his friend with a grateful ear-to-ear smile. He had given up his own Saturday—and pizza plans—to lend a hand to his friend's family. This altruistic gesture is characteristic of the *volersi bene*, that special love, between close Italian friends. The men worked side by side until almost midnight and then again on Sunday morning until they completed the *vendemmia*, the grape harvesting and winemaking process, for Vincenzo's parents. In *Italia*, friendship is the same whether you travel north or south: no matter what you need or when you need it, a friend is someone who makes himself available— not only to you, but also to your family.

You may not live close to your friend's parents, but if you live near your friend, you probably live near their children and spouse too. How about lending a hand the next time your friend's family wants to have a tag sale? Why not offer to drive her children to school the week her car is at the mechanic's? What about you and your partner offering a hand when your friend's spouse announces he is going to repaint the garage? There are many ways to give new meaning to the term "family friends"!

Approaching friendship with your heart and soul

If you're going to invest your time and emotional resources in friendship, why not make it really count by giving it your enthusiasm as well? Openly show your friends how delighted you are to be with them! Put animation into your interactions. Show your whole range of wonderful human emotions as you feel them in your heart.

Last spring I was inspired to sit for a minute in the courtyard of Parma's renowned Battistero and drink in a bit of the atmosphere around me. It was dusk, and the sky was a beautiful pink and gray. Pigeons clustered on the cobblestones at the feet of each new person who sat on the steps of the church or on the stone benches along the sides. I closed my eyes to dream for a moment but was abruptly summoned to reality by the strong lively voices of two young women on the bench alongside of me.

"Ma che ti succede, sei matta?" But what's happened to you, are you crazy?

The voices became steadily louder and shriller, and before long even the pigeons decided the wait for food wasn't worth the aggravation, and moved on. I was sure the first punch would be thrown any time now as the argument continued to heat up and hands flew in a gestured expression that I wouldn't dare repeat. Since gesturing is not as acceptable in the north as it is in the south, I knew this could be serious. I made another attempt to close my eyes and block out the drama next to me. Then, like magic, the fight ended as abruptly as it began. The two friends were hugging, laughing, and holding each other's hands with glee. However volatile this exchange might have seemed to an outsider, I knew that between friends in Italy, it was a sign of total involvement in the sheer pleasure of being together. There was joy, disagreement, physical closeness, and a whole range of emotions, but not a second of looking around distractedly out of boredom while the other one spoke.

I closed my eyes again, and smiled. Ah, the simple delight of the company of a friend!

chapter three

The Unabashed
Joy of Romance

Oh blessed be the day, the month, the year,
the season and the time, the hour, the instant,
the gracious countryside, the place where I was
struck by those two lovely eyes that bound me.
—Francesco Petrarca (English translation)

Viva l'amore, long live love! In a land that transforms men into poets who bless the day, month, year, season, time, and countryside where they first laid eyes on their ladylove, you can't help but wonder if romance wasn't an Italian invention to begin with! Where else would semi-nude billboard images blend in so casually with the natural scenery? Where else could you openly admire the beauty of detailed sculptures of the nude human body and not raise an eyebrow? In what other culture would a national supermodel offer to strip if her favorite soccer team won the national championship? Romance in the boot-shaped Oz is everywhere and everything. It is a part of its history, literature, art, and music. It is a good meal over a candlelit dinner, or a jaunt to the public museum, where lovers go scurrying into private corners to have a moment alone. Romance is the unexpected interlude that just happens when you are gathering wild mushrooms in the woods. It is the middle-aged widower who looks in the mirror with newfound passion in his soul. For Italians, love is as natural and vital to life as breathing.

Intimacy is extremely important to Italians, but perhaps what we find most seductive about the *bel paese* is its sensuous romantic aura. From the breathless finesse of a Rudolph Valentino to the ultimate sacrifices of Romeo and Juliet, for most of us Italy signifies love and romance. It is where men sing shamelessly about the emotional torture of unrequited love. It is where women smile flirtatiously, fully aware of their elevated status in the hearts of Italian men. In the *bel paese,* romance is as natural an expression as eating a spaghetti dinner, and one approaches it with the same gusto and frequency. Italians will talk to you about their love lives without the slightest embarrassment. It is a land whose people like to get up close.

While our culture may be less openly demonstrative, this does not mean we have to live without romance! You don't have to live in Italy in order to live a life of Italian-style passion. As with anything worthwhile, romance takes a bit of effort, but once you make it habit, it will be yours for as long as you keep inviting it into your life. My maternal grandparents were madly in love until the day my grandmother died. Their lives were filled with hugs and kisses and heated arguments that led to passionate making up. When I read books that say romance can't last past the first few years, I think: these authors should have known my grandparents—the experience would have made them change their theories.

So if you are ready to roll up your sleeves and begin, we'll get started right away on the five indispensable *dolce vita* prescriptions for putting romance into *your* life—and outsmarting the psychology books that say it can't last forever:

1. Like who you are.
2. Stay positive.
3. Be open to love.
4. Be male/be female.
5. Make romance a daily habit.

Like who you are.

If you were questioned whether you love yourself, you would probably be quick to reply with a resounding "Yes!" But what if I asked if you *like* yourself? That question is a bit harder for many of us. Once, I stood at the counter of a little sandwich bar in Padova, eating my *tramezzino*, sandwich, and watching the local passersby through the large glass storefront window in front of me. I couldn't help but marvel at the way these people carried themselves—with much the same confidence you would see in movie stars. Their well-dressed bodies were held tall, and they acknowledged each other with strong eye contact and immense smiles. The total impression was that of "I like me."

Italians don't just walk down the street—they perform! It is not a phony show, but rather a manifestation of a strong self-acceptance that is impenetrable by any external force. Liking who you are comes through in everything you do. In reality, your life's greatest mission may be making yourself into a person that you truly like. Once you like yourself, you can love joyfully and without diminishing your own self-reserves. You will be ready to open your arms wide and let romance in. You will also be able to say no to experiences that don't feed in to your positive self-image. Self-likers are passion-magnets. As an old Italian proverb states, *Chi vuol farsi amare, amabile deve diventare,* if you want to be loved, you have to make yourself lovable. You must start with you!

There are a few *bel paese* points to cover on the road to self-like. You must try your best to:

❦ Let go of old baggage.
❦ Develop a strong sense of self.
❦ Set boundaries.
❦ Use upbeat body language.

Let go of old baggage.
The field of psychology emphasizes the importance of childhood and adolescent development for good reason. These periods of your life have more to do with shaping your identity than any other stages in your lifespan. If you don't reach adulthood with a healthy and positive self-identity, it will be difficult to share yourself with another person in a romantic relationship until you do.

My friend Luana from Piacenza uses the analogy of money in the bank. "If you don't have anything in your account, you can only give loans to the person you are trying to love. On the surface, it looks like you are loving them back, but before long you become deeply indebted and start to become needy. Neediness does to romance what pesticide does to bugs."

Hardly any of us goes through childhood and adolescence unscathed, at least to some degree. What can you do if you don't like who you are today because of negative feedback you got when you were younger? Instead of clinging to your past and using it as an excuse, it is important to start doing things that make you feel better about yourself right now.

Romance doesn't go looking for people who are full of hang-ups. Unresolved negativity prevents you from making deposits in your personal bank account. As a result, you risk becoming stingy or needy and lacking in the abundance your heart needs in order to be generous in romance.

Recovering from past hurts makes you whole and psychologically ready to love. Rather than calling this process "healing," I call it "whole-ing," because, essentially, you are taking the fragments of your past and piecing them back together so that you can complete and start liking yourself. A self-liking individual doesn't hand the burden of his past over to his lover to fix. That kind of behavior will drain a relationship in a very short time.

The whole-ing process starts when you stop dwelling on past hurts and start doing what it takes to put the fragments back together. Here are three approaches, in increasing intensity, that will help you put your feelings into words and resolve problems.

1. Telling you to **keep a journal** seems almost cliché, since it is advocated for everything from losing weight to healing lower back pain. However, no matter how clichéd it is, it works. In letting go of your past hurts, journaling is a form of self-education. It allows you to learn and respond to your own needs and issues. You might ask a question and not be able to write down the answer for days, but sooner or later that answer will come. Most of the things we need to know are right inside us the whole time.

2. Sometimes a **good long talk with a close friend** is the best psychotherapy there is. Try to share ideas about what it is you are holding on to from the past and how it is affecting your life in a negative way today. Assure your friend that you will return the favor when he/she needs to talk to you.

3. If you feel that issues from your past are too overpowering a task to figure out by journaling or talking with a friend, **make an appointment with a mental health professional**. They will help guide you through your journey and point things out that you might not be able to see on your own.

In completing the whole-ing process, you need to do more than put feelings into words. You also have to come up with an action plan as to how you are going to change past patterns from here on out. So what is your action plan? Express it. Talk about it. Write it down. Sometimes all you will need to do is change small individual behaviors, like my friend Sylvia did.

Whenever Sylvia's boyfriend used to tell her that he liked a certain color she was wearing, or a certain style garment, she felt the hair stand up on the back of her neck!

"I heard my mother's voice criticizing me all over again! 'Sylvia,' she would say, 'Go change your sweater; that color makes you look pale.' It took me a while to realize that Attilio wasn't criticizing me. In fact, he was giving me a compliment by telling me I looked great when I wore certain things! Once I realized why I was reacting the way I was, I started to use the pinch technique. I would pinch myself as a reminder to stop and think before I responded to Attilio. Was I taking this in the right way? Was I letting some old records replay in my head? When I got the hang of stopping myself and switching gears, I was able to appreciate his comments and not spoil the evening with unfounded hurt feelings. This person was really saying something nice to me!"

Develop a strong sense of self.
Lucio was an artist and poet whom a friend of mine met in Italy when she was 19 years old. He was several years younger than Joanna, and at that age it mattered! Thus the idea of a romantic relationship hadn't even occurred to her. One day, as he was giving her a walking tour of the backroads of his town, he stopped suddenly and planted his lips on hers with a Fabio-like passion that might have graced the cover of a romance novel. When she finally caught her breath and figured out what had happened, Joanna nicely explained that she had a boyfriend back home. That was OK with him, he said.

Eventually she returned to the States, he stayed in Italy, and life returned to normal. A few weeks later, she began to receive the first of what would be bi-monthly installments of incredibly beautiful poetry—with a theme of unrequited love. The poems were exquisite expressions of feeling, with the more "tortured" sentiments either underlined two or three times or written in a different color ink, usually red. Several years later, Joanna informed Lucio she was getting married. He was surprisingly serene on the phone and wished her well. Shortly afterward, he announced plans of his own marriage. In the letter was a short note expressing his gratitude for giving him the experience of unreturned love. "It was a great period of time for me artistically," Lucio wrote. "My paintings and poetry just flowed from the emotion I felt from your rejection!"

Lucio was not a shallow person. In fact, he was quite sincere in his pursuit of my friend, but emotionally healthy enough to be able to see his "misfortune" as an opportunity for artistic growth instead of the end of the world, as his poetic words would have suggested. I have heard this theme expressed many times in Italian circles, where the belief is that whatever might happen in life, it is important to keep one's dignity and move on because "Love will always find you again."

Set boundaries.

You will feel instantly better about yourself the moment you start to say no and set limits with people who ask more from you than you want to give. The key in setting boundaries is to be clear and consistent without being rude or offensive—which will make you feel worse instead of better. The broken record technique works wonders. I once heard Salvatore, a pizza maker in Sorrento, use it when a friend came in to ask him to make a special pizza during his busiest time.

"I can't," said Sal. "If you want what I have here you can take it, but if you want it made special you have to wait until the lunch rush is over in about an hour and a half, then give it time to cook."

"What? Sali', *dai,* come on! I can't wait, I need the pizza now; I've got my mother-in-law and her family in the car. Can't you throw it together and we'll come back in a half hour when we finish shopping?"

"I'm swamped right now and have no help. I would do it if I could, but I can't right now."

"*Ti prego,* please!"

"*Ehi, non oggi*, not today!"

"Forty-five minutes?"

"No, no."

"*Uffá*, come on! All right, all right, then make it after your lunch rush, and I'll be back for it a couple of hours, OK?"

"Sure. That I can do. I'll put on some extra *basilico*, basil, just the way you like."

Everyone was eventually happy with this outcome. Boundaries tell people you respect yourself and that they must respect you too.

Use upbeat body language.

Italians are very attentive to how they carry themselves. I once watched two strangers standing at opposite ends of a café counter in Milan. She was a beautiful, tall blonde with lips that were lined, frosted, glossed, and then some. At the other end of the counter stood her admirer; every wave in his tousled locks intentional, drinking his espresso with the finesse of a movie star. She tossed her long bangs to the side with a sexy movement of her head as her polished lips broke into a slight smile. Using only a hand gesture, he ordered a pastry to be brought to her place. She motioned him over with her pointer finger, "You will have to help me eat this, it is way too large." For a few seconds their only communication was a smile. Whether or not they got together for a romantic interlude afterward is anyone's guess, but what most impressed me was the romantic power of self-assured body language.

Reflecting confidence in your body language tells the world you like who you are. There is something to be said for standing up straight, looking others in the eye, and smiling. That is usually all it takes to send the right romantic signal. Did you ever notice how many people walk down the street with their eyes averted, or with their heads down? Sometimes their shoulders are hunched over as if trying to enclose themselves into a shell. While it may be that sometimes people just want to think and don't want their thoughts interrupted, more often they are simply afraid to make eye contact with another person. Insecure body language tells the world you feel shy, timid, or unworthy.

If your body language does not come across with attitude, try using the mirror technique. Each morning, before you head out the door, look into a full-length mirror and correct your body language. Look directly at your reflection, as if it were someone else, and smile. Make it the biggest, broadest smile you can muster without looking goofy or insincere. Next, check out your posture. Imagine a length of string running from the top of your head to the ceiling. Gently roll your shoulders backward and down. Hold your stomach in and tuck your tailbone so as to position your hips in a slight pelvic tilt. Now practice walking a few steps. Keep your head up and your gaze out. Put a smile on your face and swing your arms confidently. Keep rehearsing until your body says, "I like me, and I am ready to like you, too!" Take a mental snapshot of this mirror image and take it with you during the day as a reminder.

Stay Positive.

Romance finds positive people. It practically sniffs them out and digs wherever it has to to get at them because, in short, romance is attracted to energy similar to itself. You'll notice that when you are positive it seems like a million people want to be around you. In contrast, not even the dog wants to be around you when you're moping or complaining!

Leonardo was a middle-age bachelor that I knew from the old neighborhood. He was not particularly good-looking, although he was always meticulously dressed. He spoke English with a thick Italian accent and carried himself like royalty. I was enchanted by his little package store, to which, surprisingly, more female customers than male flocked each day. That was unusual for that period of time, when most of the liquor buyers were men! As a kid, I would go into Leonardo's now and again when I could scrape up the ten cents it cost for a bottle of soda. On one particular day, it dawned on me that the women in Leonardo's store were not there to buy liquor. It seems one had come to bring him a dish of cookies; another to let him know about some information she found that might interest him; and yet another to see how his cold had been coming along. I was way too young to know what magnetic attraction was all about, but Leonardo could have written the book on it. I noticed how he talked to the women who came to see him, how he complimented them on their hairdos or their sweaters. He would look into each woman's eyes as she spoke, as if there were no one else in the room. He ended every conversation on a positive note. Even if someone had mentioned a person who had just died, Leonardo would comment about how wonderful that person was while alive.

Leo's positive personality wasn't reserved for his female customers alone. He had a smile and a good word for everyone who peeked their head into the store to say *"come va"*, how is it going? He honestly always saw the glass as half-full. That is the real secret of attraction. Leo's positive outlook attracted more romance into his life than most of us would even know what to do with! Leo, like most Italians, didn't believe in putting on a phony smile. Italians will complain quite colorfully at the opportune time, but then, after a good *sfogo*, venting, they're done with it. Thus, negativity doesn't get in the way of recognizing and appreciating what is good about life. While most of us don't need to be told how to express our negative emotions, some of us can use help with recognizing and expressing the positive ones! Here are a few *bel paese* tips to infuse your own personality with a luminous energy:

❦ Let yourself be happy.
❦ Learn to argue with yourself.
❦ Stay interesting.
❦ Show enthusiasm.

Let yourself be happy.
There are a million small ways to be happy, and none of them require waiting X number of years in order to reach this or that goal. For John, it might be a good home-cooked meal; for Fern it might be a peaceful walk in the park. But one thing is true about personal happiness: romance is stifled and suffocated without it. Romance is a happy state and people feel inspired to act romantic when their hearts are light. How do you make yourself be happy even if you don't feel happy now?

From what the research tells us, happiness is not an endpoint; it is a process. When you are engaged in doing the things you love to do, you lose all sense of time. Those are the times you are immersed in the process of happiness. Up until now, you might have thought that happiness had to be defined in the future tense. Italians don't hang around waiting for a million Euros to fall from the sky—they like to be happy *now*. They are happy with a dish of spaghetti, with a *passeggiata*, walk through the center of town, an afternoon *caffè*, cup of coffee, with a friend. The key is to be aware of the processes that make you happy. Then engage in them often.

In addition to being able to recognize joyful moments, happiness thrives on laughter. Expose yourself often to the experiences and activities that strike your funny bone. Italians, for instance, love to tell each other jokes. Of course, some of their favorite jokes pertain to love and romance, and some of them can get quite *osè*, risqué.

Learn to argue with yourself.
In the field of psychology, it is a well-known fact that when we feel defeated, we tend to exaggerate the negativity and make ourselves depressed. For example, if someone I ask for a date turns me down, I start thinking that person must really find me repulsive. For that matter, maybe I'm a loser in love in general. Oh, and now that I think of it, I haven't been doing so hot in other areas of my life either!

Do you see how irrational our thinking can be? Worse yet, irrational negativity is a recursive cycle, which, if not broken, can snowball into a full-blown depression. Let me tell you what my grandfather Domenico used to do when he felt down or disappointed about something. He argued with himself! Today, thanks to psychologists like Albert Ellis and Martin Seligman, we have nailed down the art of self-arguing to a science for combating depression. Domenico didn't know any of that back then. He just instinctively looked at the evidence, and if it didn't give him a good enough reason to be depressed, then he was going to concentrate on the positive, and that was that.

Let's reconsider the dating example I used above. How would I argue myself out of negativity? I would start by looking for evidence that my negative statements are true: Do I have any proof that this person found me repulsive? Has everyone I have ever asked out refused me? Is everything else really going bad in my life—or are there some good things that are happening to me too? Once you have given some rationality to your thought process, you will calm down and feel happier as things are put into their proper perspective.

Stay interesting.
It is one thing to exchange flirty glances or send mystery pastries to someone in a coffee shop. Once the romance is initiated, however, it must have substance in order to keep it going, or else things will get boring awfully fast. I tell people there is a rather simple way to make themselves interesting: read the daily newspaper from cover to cover every single day. That's it. Of course, you can do other things if you want to and if you have the time. You can take adult-education courses, or go to seminars or lectures that interest you on topics that you want to learn about, but you really don't have to. Reading the newspaper will give you something to say. It will give you knowledge, help you form opinions, and keep you interesting.

Show enthusiasm.

A friend of mine recently joined a dating service. The service guaranteed her at least two "contacts" a month. These prospects were to call her and on the phone they would arrange a meeting place for their first date. The first caller turned her off immediately. "No way on Earth!" she wailed. "His voice was monotone and he seemed to have about as much interest in meeting in person as a vegetarian would have in chomping down on a steak."

"What did he say?" I asked

"Well for one thing, every time I suggested a place or time to meet, he answered 'I don't care.' Can you believe it? Well if he didn't care, neither should I."

I understood my friend's point. While sometimes aloofness or emotional distance is caused by shyness, it often comes across as indifference. Lack of enthusiasm does to romance what bug repellent does to a mosquito—it repels it! When you are with someone you feel attracted to, let your enthusiasm show in your voice, in your words, and in your gestures. Focus on the positive parts of your day. Talk in an optimistic way. Be enthusiastic about your life. There is no greater people repellant than a depressed, anxious, or angry demeanor.

Be open to love.

The key is to be open—not desperate. If you go hunting love with a shotgun, I guarantee you will only scare it away. My friend Tony was so desperate to find love after his divorce that he unwittingly sent out vibes that scared away any woman within one hundred miles of him. I tried to tell him that romance is like dessert. If you are needy, you should be working on the main meal. That means learn how to fulfill yourself first, and when that happens, you will be ready for your dessert. Tony didn't see it that way. He thought that unless he had a partner, his life was meaningless. Think about what an ominous burden it is for someone to feel he or she is required to give your life meaning! The trick is to be open to love without obsessing. What does that mean? It means do things that put you in contact with other available people, but make sure they are things you like to do anyway. Don't sit home all the time and then lament if your phone doesn't ring. You have to put yourself in the running or you can't win.

If you already have a partner, you are ahead of the game. All you need to do to be open to romance is know how to recognize, appreciate, and acknowledge your lover's romantic gestures. Then give freely of yourself, using your instinct as a guide. At times, that may mean one or the other of you is giving more. While the embers of romance die quickly by an "eye for an eye" mentality, it is important to assess whether the totality of your relationship is balanced and reciprocal.

Where can you go to find love if you are unattached? No, you don't have to go to Italy. On the contrary, research shows that similarity breeds attraction—so you can relax and look around your own backyard. You will, however, have a better chance for lasting romance if you at least agree on important values. Beyond that, there are a couple of techniques Italians use in enhancing their chances for passion, which work well in just about any culture.

❦ Let the arts inspire romance.
❦ Make the first move.

Let the arts inspire romance.

Years ago, when I was a student in Perugia, I remember sitting at the fountain *Fontana Maggiore* in the center of the town and reading one of my textbook assignments. The day was sunny, warm, and clear, and the fluttering of pigeon wings almost lulled me to sleep at regular intervals. During one of these lapses I felt someone tap my shoulder and I jumped.

"Ciao!" he said with a great wide smile. Daniele, a young Italian student about the same age as I, sat on the fountain wall alongside me with a large artist pad and pens in his arms.

"Ciao," I said, introducing myself. Daniele told me he was studying to be a medical artist, and he showed me his collection of lungs, liver, kidneys, and other organs I couldn't quite identify. Before I could comment on any of them, he drew the cap off of his pen and began to sketch something with lightning speed. I watched as the form of a human heart began to take shape. No, it wasn't the type of heart one sends to a lover on Valentine's Day. This one came complete with blood, veins, and arteries, but right at the bottom were the words *A Rachele, con il sorriso incantevole,* To Raeleen, with the enchanting smile.

Although I never saw Daniele after that, I kept his sketch for years. To me it represented the power of romance, wherever and however it finds you. Just a simple tender gesture, even if it leads to nothing more, has the ability to lift the spirits and make a person feel glad to be alive!

If you need a little romantic inspiration, do what the Italians do: turn to the arts to put you in the mood. Try going to the museum to admire humanistic paintings and sculptures. Listen to your favorite classical concertos or contemporary love ballads. Read some enticingly romantic poetry. Sometimes we forget how the arts add necessary balance and dimension to our souls. But even if romance doesn't turn you into a poet yourself, reading love poetry will get you in the mood nevertheless. Consider, for example, the words that Dante Alighieri (1265–1321) wrote of his Beatrice. They are simple yet hauntingly profound:

> *L'amore e' soltanto una luce che brilla nello sguardo*
> *di Beatrice, uno splendore che nasce dall'anima e*
> *si rivela prima negli occhi, poi nel sorriso.*
> *(Love is but a light that shines in Beatrice's look;*
> *a splendor that is born of the soul and reveals*
> *itself first in her eyes, then in her smile.)*
> —FROM "NE LI OCCHI PORTA LA MIA DONNA AMORE"

The more exposure you have to the human expression of romance, the more you will feel like opening your own heart up for passion. Remember that romance doesn't have to be logical; it only has to be enjoyed. For Italians, love exists for its own sake and needs no defense of its existence.

In the words of Italian writer Carlo Fornari, in writing about Maria Luigia, the one-time duchess of Parma, in "Maria Luigia: A love of a woman":

> *If we knew her better, perhaps we would have loved her less: In order*
> *for love to be blind, enduring, and selfless, it must also be irrational,*
> *and uncontaminated by useless psychological analyses or moral judg-*
> *ments, that more times than not end up becoming prejudicial.*

Make the first move.

If you were to sit on the Spanish Steps in Rome and observe native Roman male-female interactions, you would discover that romance knows no embarrassment. When a person feels romantic in Italy, the world knows about it. It may involve a gaze so intense it mentally undresses someone, or a delicate brush of the arm in conversation that leaves no doubt about one's desires. Electrically-charged harmless flirtation between the sexes is neither interpreted as sexual harassment nor as loose morality among those living in the Italian culture. It is merely an affirmation of life. Without sensuality, one day would blend into the next and life would become flat and unromantic.

Interessante!
The Italian language distinguishes friends from lovers with the ti voglio bene *and the* ti amo *ways of saying, "I love you." The former is for friends and family, the latter is distinctly for lovers. Likewise, friends and lovers don't confuse their roles.*

If you want romance in your life, do what the Italians do: take a chance and send out the first signal. Now and then, you are bound to get a welcoming response! It is also important to be receptive to romantic cues if they come from someone you are interested in. Romance is hit or miss, but half the fun is the potential for a satisfying "hit."

Katherine, for example, met Aldo through the Internet one night when she entered an Italian chat room to ask about an old song her grandfather used to sing to her. Aldo not only knew the song

Katherine was looking for, but as it turned out, it was a tune that originated in his hometown of Asti, which, coincidentally, was where Katherine's grandfather grew up. The two formed a pretty nice friendship through emails and virtual chats, discussing everything from local recipes to regional history. Like most Italians, Aldo was well-versed historically, and loved to talk about his local traditions. To Katherine, it was like reconnecting with her roots. They soon began talking on the telephone, and after a year of constant correspondence, Katherine decided to take the first step and look up Aldo when she went to Italy that spring to search for her distant relatives. Aldo was thrilled to meet her in person and turned out to be a real *romanticone,* romantic. He took her to castles where they picnicked on bread, cheese, and wine. They drove up the mountains and spent hours sharing the breathtaking panorama. He brought her to cathedrals, where they lit candles for the people in their lives who needed prayers. They shared *gelato,* ice cream, while walking through the streets of her grandfather's native town. To this day, Katherine wonders what her life would be like had she not taken the first step toward romance. She and Aldo have been now been married for more than seven years.

Be Male/Be Female

Italians believe that their God-given masculine/feminine differences have a right to coexist and be openly cherished! In Italy, men hold doors for their women. They carry their bags and help them with their coats. They gaze into their loved one's eyes over dinner and bite their lower lips with impatience for the moment when they will be alone.

Women, likewise, are unapologetic about letting their sensuality shine through in their gestures, in their dress, and in their receptivity of the male overture. They smile sweetly and move with grace, as if they deserve to be treasured. Italian men and women appreciate the inherent sexual prowess of the other and they are also proud of their own natural sensuality.

Lorena is sixty-five years old and owns a little dry cleaning business in Verona. When you walk into her store you will catch a gentle whiff of *Violetta di Parma*, Parma's specialty violet perfume, in subtle competition with the chemical cleaning fumes. Her hair and makeup look as if she planned everything out the night before. Her lipstick matches her nail polish, which matches the lavender floral of her hand-embroidered sweater. This senior *signora* wears higher heels than I have even personally attempted. Her eyes are subtly lined in deep lavender, and she wears a tastefully faint blush that gives her the look of a woman fifteen years her junior. Male customers love bringing their shirts to Lorena because she always gives them that special care and treats the shirts as if they were her babies. Now and then she gives a playful wink as she hands the clothing back to its owner. If ever there was an exemplar of Italian femininity, Lorena wins hands down!

The most fundamental *dolce vita* approach to sensuality is to be proud of who you are and act like it!

Women really do love men who are strong, and men love women who are gentle. These qualities reflect the nature and essence of men and women, and, coincidentally, they are also what make us so attractive to the opposite sex.

The first time I saw Giulia and didn't yet know who she was, or how our paths would cross in the future, I was stopping into a *caffè*, bar, to buy a bottle of *acqua minerale*, mineral water, and a cup of java. While I was drinking my coffee, the whole place came to a sudden standstill. In walked a stately Venetian woman with blonde hair that was vaguely reminiscent of the metallic tint used by her Renaissance predecessors. She took long, graceful strides in her form-fitting leather skirt and high-heeled boots. Although the men's mouths hung to the floor, Giulia neither quickened her pace nor whipped out her cell phone to call the police. Surprisingly, she looked directly into the eyes of her admirers, gave them what looked to be a subtle smile of acknowledgment, and slunk past them as if she were on a fashion runway in Milan. Most of us can't imagine such a sexually charged scene being so innocuous, but Giulia responded to the whistles and stares as graciously as a theater performer might respond to applause.

I met Giulia again several days later, when I ended up in the emergency room of an Italian hospital with a sprained ankle. No, she wasn't just another patient sitting alongside me in the waiting room. She was the physician who examined me! This was the quintessential unity of brains, beauty, professionalism, and femininity. It was like an Italian romantic work of art.

Make romance a daily habit.

American psychologist Robert Sternberg wrote about consummate love, which is something we would all consider to be the ideal. This kind of love transcends simple romantic behaviors and involves elements of intimacy (closeness and sharing), passion (physical attraction) and commitment (long-term promise). Consummate love is the most complete type of love, and yet it is the hardest to attain.

To see my grandparents together, you would have thought they were married yesterday, although in reality they had been married for more than fifty years. While romance was just a small part of their deep commitment to each other, it still had its place in their relationship throughout the years. When they fought, they fought respectfully and always made sure the fighting ended when the last word was said. When they were with others, they would always share a united front, no matter what their individual opinions were. Every Saturday afternoon, she would make his favorite platter of fried potatoes with a sprinkling of salt. Every first of the month, he would run up the stairs after the shoe wholesaler made his delivery to let her see the first pair of a new style that had just come in. When they talked, their hands inevitably landed on parts of the other's arm or shoulder, or one would lean toward the other to listen while he or she spoke. On occasion, there were special winks that only the other person understood. They always talked about what was on their minds and, above all, they really enjoyed doing things together.

I learned a lot from watching my grandparents. I noted particular techniques they used and that you can use too if you want to create a lifelong romance with the person you love:

❦ Avoid the four poisons of romance
❦ Appreciate each other's style
❦ Six weeks to a romance habit

Avoid the four poisons of romance

There is nothing that kills romance more permanently than:

1. Complaining
2. Criticizing
3. Fighting ugly
4. The inability to forgive

If you relate to your partner in any of these ways, or even think you might, please drag out that journal right now and figure out your trigger points. What is the thing you complain about the most regarding your partner? What are the situations, or the things he or she says that cause you to criticize? What personal attacks usually surface when you argue? How long does it usually take you to talk things out and resolve the issue?

Since problem-solving is always a two-part process, it is never enough to simply pinpoint the problem and determine what triggered it. You must also figure out a way to learn from the problem and then do things differently. Learning from our mistakes doesn't mean beating ourselves up about them, although a heartfelt apology with an action plan for doing better next time does wonders to smoothe things over and get a fresh start.

My grandparents were always careful about what they said to each other. Even in the heat of an argument, you could tell they knew where to draw the line. Nonna confirmed this to me one day when she said, "Words are something we can never take back."

Appreciate each other's style
No two people are identical in romance. I may like to say "I love you"
one hundred times a day. You might not enjoy saying "I love you" at
all, but you massage my feet every night after supper. Differences in
romantic expression are what keep things interesting, and it is important to keep them in the proper perspective. You can't simply demand
that someone else relate to you in the identical way you relate to him
or her. That is not only unrealistic, it also boring and meaningless.
Think about it. If I demand you tell me you love me a certain number of times a day, how much depth would those words really carry?
Instead, if I could interpret your foot massages as the equivalent of my
"I love you"s, then romance would thrive on its own terms.

Six weeks to a romance habit
Since it takes about six weeks to build a new habit, how about drawing
up a six-week plan for romance? Think of a few little things you can do
each week that will either bring a smile to your loved one's face or help
you to draw new romance into your life. Make sure they are things you
are willing to do regularly and that you feel good about doing.

Social psychologist David Myers found that people in stable, loving
relationships enjoy greater well-being, whether they are young or old,
male or female, rich or poor. This conclusion is affirmed by both
American and European survey research. People are simply more satisfied with life when they know how to give and receive love. Those
who say they are satisfied with their marriages report feeling less lonely
and depressed than people who are either not in stable relationships
or are in marriages that cause stress and negativity. Making an effort

to put daily romance into your relationship is like the difference between fertilizing your flower garden and leaving its survival up to chance. Romance is what first attracts us to each other, and we should never lose sight of the power it has to keep us together. Romance comprises the gestures that add spice to life and show a person they are important to you. Unabashed romance is what gives Italian relationships—and possibly yours too—that sweet touch of durability, irrationality, selflessness, and blindness to fault.

chapter four

✦

Meals that Nourish the
Body and Soul

*There is nothing quite like the quiet lull that descends on this other-
wise crowded, noisy, chaotic city when the* ora di pranzo
*(lunchtime)…is upon the populace. Rome seems empty. Most stores
close. People vanish. And the only sounds you hear as you pass
through…are the particular rhythms of plates clacking, silverware
clinking, and linen snapping on the tables outside the restaurants…or
from the open windows of the palazzi, where families have gathered
as they have for more than two millennia to break bread.*

—ALAN EPSTEIN, *AS THE ROMANS DO*

From a young age, I recognized that coming together at our Italian
family dinner table, *a tavola*, was something far more significant than
simply putting fork to mouth. It was an experience that eventually
formed the foundation of everything we would become in life. It was
there that we learned how to eat right, how to think right, how to
relate to others, and how to stay emotionally and physically healthy.
We learned social skills at the dinner table. We learned about life. The
dinner table gave us security and nourishment. It was a consistent
focal point of our day that provided support, good nutrition, and a
sense of camaraderie. At the table, we learned gratitude for what we
had and the importance of giving something back to the world. That

is no small task for such a commonplace event as eating dinner.

Often our dinner table would be doubled—we would put two tables together and invite grandparents, aunts, uncles, or very special friends. On those occasions, it was more of a party than an intimate gathering, and the food would be even more exquisite than usual because everyone brought their specialty dishes or desserts. Music, laughter, and the happy clinking of tableware would fill the air, leaving all of us with a sense that the world was a magnificent place.

Today, I maintain the integrity of *la tavola italiana,* the Italian table, for my own family and friends, and hopefully my children will want to carry on the tradition for generations after me. You don't have to be Italian to bring that life-affirming *bel paese* ambience to your own dinner table. Just start with these four tips for creating an eating experience that nourishes body and soul in the tradition passed down to me from my own Italian family:

1. Consider a nutritious Mediterranean menu.
2. It is not only what you eat that counts, but also how you eat.
3. Make mealtime a social experience.
4. Start with some basic supplies and simple recipes.

Consider a nutritious Mediterranean menu.

The other day a television commercial was plugging the Mediterranean diet in a pill. This modern-day miracle promised to give us the benefits of red wine without having to drink red wine; the benefits of fresh fish without having to eat fish; and the benefits of olive oil, fruits, and vegetables without having to consume those either. The only thing the manufacturer hadn't figured out yet was how to put about two hours of family interaction time into that pill.

As absurd as the commercial was, the benefits of the Mediterranean way of eating are far from a new discovery. In the 1950s, nutrition researcher Ancel Keys conducted a longitudinal study in which he followed the progress of twelve thousand participants between the ages of forty and sixty from various countries, including Japan, the U.S., Holland, Yugoslavia, Finland, and Italy. He found that some diseases were characteristic of more industrial societies, where people consumed excessive amounts of fat, carbohydrates, and proteins. In addition to the benefits of olive oil, the Mediterranean, or "poor man's", diet based on southern Italian cuisine, consisted of cereals, greens, fruit, and fish, which reduces cholesterol and the risk of cardiovascular diseases, particularly atherosclerosis, hypertension, heart attack, and stroke. A Mediterranean Food Pyramid is located in the back of this book for your reference. There is also research showing that this type of eating is beneficial to patients with Type II diabetes.

Simplicity and purity are the most important components in Italian cuisine. Italy has always taken vigilant measures to keep its food

Interessante!

Parmigiano-Reggiano is a hard, textured cheese, cooked but not pressed. It is made from the raw milk of cows that have been fed only grass or hay. The only additive permitted is salt, and the aging process lasts an average of two years.

chemical-free and non-genetically engineered. Despite the fact that most Italians couldn't tell you directly what "organic" food is, almost fifty thousand Italian companies are engaged in producing it—which constitutes 40 percent of the European Union total, according to the Coldiretti Research Firm, making Italy the most organic country in the European Union! In addition to starting with the best ingredients, these ingredients are also combined in a way that maximizes longevity and vitality, according to the results of a study developed by the World Health Organization scientists. The Disability-Adjusted Life Expectancy (DALE) study analyzed longevity in the equivalent of "full health" across ninety-one countries throughout the world. Italy came in fifth, as compared to the U.S.'s ranking of twenty-fourth under this system. One of the reasons cited for the disappointing U.S. rank was the high level of coronary heart disease in this country. Could it be that the Mediterranean style of eating really protects people from heart disease and cancer? Many presumed this to be the case, but until a Saint-Etienne School of Medicine study there was some doubt as to whether other variables—such as genes or exercise habits—may have confused findings from previous studies comparing the Mediterranean diet with the Northern European and American eating styles.

The French study confirmed the benefits of following a Mediterranean approach to nutrition. They randomly divided 605 heart attack survivors into two groups. One group worked in conjunction with their doctors to follow a diet similar to the American Heart Association (AHA) dietary regimen, and the other group followed a Mediterranean style of eating. The emphasis was less on cutting fat—as in the AHA's 30 percent limit—and more on choosing such foods as fruits, vegetables, grains, and fish and substituting olive oil for butter.

Significant differences between the two groups were found during the following four years. In the group following a Mediterranean eating plan, fourteen members died, in contrast to the AHA group in which the death rate was twenty-four. Also, the Mediterranean diet group had less than half as many cancers and one-third the number of heart attacks as the AHA group. Researchers speculated that the Mediterranean diet might have had better results because people are more likely to stick to a diet that tastes so good. Also, the omega-3 fatty acids from fish and olive oil—which are found in Mediterranean menus—have been shown to lower heart disease and cancer rates in laboratory animals.

While no one denies the influence of genetics in heart disease and cancer, researchers now believe that dietary factors can play a key role in preventing them and extending longevity in existing cases. You will note on the pyramid the monthly intake of red meat and the weekly— not daily—consumption of sweets. Interestingly, at the very foundation of the pyramid, you will note that exercise is also a daily component of the healthy Mediterranean lifestyle.

For years we were told that fat was our enemy and food manufacturers saw a marvelous opportunity in fat-free desserts. What we never understood fully was the wrath of the substance that substituted for the banished grease—sugar! Experts are now discovering that excessive sugar not only promotes obesity and dental cavities, but it can also create or at least aggravate other debilitating conditions. Excessive sugar turns to fat, fosters acidity, and can trigger a general immune system breakdown. Some experts link sugar to precancerous or cancerous conditions. Fortunately, after a good Italian meal, the desire for sweets is minimal. Italians prefer a nice piece of fruit, which refreshes the palate instead of weighing you down, like a heavy piece of cake might. Rich desserts are typically served on special occasions and eaten only in small amounts. Italians don't like to snack in between meals, and you won't find them munching on cookies, candy bars, or potato chips. When food is nutritious and satisfying, the desire to eat indiscriminately throughout the day disappears.

Of course there is such a thing as consuming too much fat, and even olive oil can be overconsumed. However, the Italian philosophy of *non esagerare*, nothing exaggerated or to excess, applies to eating as well as it does to the rest of life. Since the Mediterranean diet emphasizes making healthy food choices rather than counting calories, it is always a good idea to keep a conscious eye on the portions and amount of fat you consume daily. Experts recommend total fat reduction along with increased physical activity and the cessation of smoking for overall good health. The Mediterranean diet in general emphasizes the following percentages:

$$
\left\{
\begin{array}{ll}
\textit{Carbohydrates} & \textit{55-60\%} \\
\textit{Protein} & \textit{12-15\%} \\
\textit{Fat} & \textit{25-30\%}
\end{array}
\right\}
$$

It is not only what you eat that counts, but also how you eat.

A colleague of mine once flew into New York from Florence to discuss my psychological study on body image disorders and obesity levels between the U.S. and Italy. In the middle of explaining my statistical analyses, the professor flashed a wide grin. I looked at him questioningly.

"*Ma guarda bene*, take a good look." He beckoned me to look around, and then began to count the number of fast food restaurants just within our line of vision alone.

"Certainly it is helpful to explore the psychology behind why people don't like their bodies," said the professor. "But it might be a bit more practical to start with eating habits. You are simply taking in too much fat and sugar, and doing it so rapidly that it probably doesn't even register in your brain that you have eaten!"

Sometimes the answer is so obvious that we don't need complicated studies and statistical analyses to figure it out. There are many times when we feel too worn out to cook, so we opt for fast food. Fortunately, getting into a *bel paese* food habit is really enjoyable and doesn't take as much effort as it would appear. Italians love simple eating, so even the most exquisite-looking dishes don't take

Interessante!
Giovanni LoCoco started Italy's first vegetarian fast food restaurant in 1996, a month after the Fiorentina steak was banned due to the mad cow disease scare. Soy burgers began to replace meat consumption, which was never high to begin with in Italy.

nearly as much time to prepare as you might imagine.

Breakfast—*prima colazione* in the *bel paese*—is a snap. There are no eggs or bacon to fry; just a nice cappuccino/caffe-latte—which is basically half coffee and half hot milk, and a couple of *biscotti*, lightly sweetened biscuits. *Pranzo*, lunch—or dinner if served as the main meal—might include a small amount of pasta, rice, or soup for the *primo piatto*, first dish; some chicken or fish for the *secondo*, second dish, with a *contorno*, side dish of vegetables and a green salad to cleanse the palate. Dessert will be some fresh fruit, and of course wine is served with the meal. *Cena*, supper, if it is not the main meal, can be a simple *panino imbottito*, stuffed roll, with a green salad and some fruit. How do Italians eat all of that food in the course of a day? *Piano piano*, very slowly!

In 1986, Dr. Carlo Petrini started Slow Food International, headquartered in the Piedmont region of northern Italy, to ensure against the homogenization of food around the world. He wanted to preserve foods that were in danger becoming extinct due to lack of interest on the part of the consumer. The objective was to make the proper production, preparation, and consumption of food a tradition that would live on forever. In reaction to the opening of Italy's first McDonald's restaurant in Rome, Petrini was determined to support regional producers and preserve local foods as well as revive and celebrate taste and the senses. Today, each national chapter sponsors local taste workshops. Another goal of the Slow Food movement is to teach children how to retrain their taste buds in order to increase their appreciation of food and the pleasures of *a tavola,* coming together at the table.

In our house, even as children, our taste buds were programmed to enjoy some of the more typical dishes in the Italian diet. We learned to relish *gnocchi* (potato and flour dumplings, served with tomato sauce or pesto); *minestrone* (vegetable tomato soup with beans, potatoes, celery and possibly scraps of leftover meat); eggplant *alla Parmigiana* (baked eggplant covered with tomato sauce and cheese); pasta *e fagioli* (macaroni prepared with canellini beans and celery); *polenta* (a cornmeal mixture that is sometimes flavored with bits of sausage or meat); and spaghetti *alle vongole* (spaghetti or linguini prepared with a light clam sauce). Today it might appear that my parents were gourmet chefs, but in reality, they never studied cooking and rarely even followed a recipe. My father enjoyed cooking as much as my mother did. They would open the refrigerator, and depending on what they found, would whip up one of the dishes mentioned above in seemingly no time at all.

The Italian kitchen at mealtime is always an inspired event. It was during the Renaissance that cooking was practically elevated to a fine art. Today, each of Italy's twenty-three regions boasts their distinct epicurean specialties, based on both *campanilismo*—local tradition—and available produce indigenous to the area. The sharpest difference in cuisine is between north and south. Italian cuisine almost takes on Austrian or French similarities the farther north you go. Tortellini stuffed with pumpkin and drizzled with crème sauce is not something you would find in Naples, but it is a traditional dish I have enjoyed many times in Emilia-Romagna. Likewise, the southern dishes are more likely to be pasta and tomato-based, as opposed to rice-based dishes such as *risotto alla milanese*, which is yellowish in color and seasoned with saffron. Naples is where you would go to eat pizza. Nowhere else will you find such a distinctive tomato, mozzarella, anchovy, and oregano pie *alla napoletana*, Neapolitan style, or pizza *marinara* topped with tomatoes, garlic, clams, mussels, and oregano. While the north tends to use butter to lubricate the pan or top its spaghetti, the south subscribes strictly to a more Mediterranean style of eating, nixing the butter in favor of olive oil—extra-virgin. The one unifying factor for this mosaic of regional mini-cultures it is *un bel bicchiere di vino*—a nice glass of wine. Whether to cleanse and refresh the palate between courses or to welcome friends to the house, Italians view moderate wine drinking as a natural, healthy tradition that "builds the blood." Even children might be allowed to take a sip of wine at mealtime, or enjoy a bite of their parents' wine-soaked fruit, such as ripe summer peaches. Often one enjoys *il vino fatto in casa*, homemade wine. Almost everyone in Italy either makes their own or knows someone who does during the early fall tradition of *la vendemmia*—the grape harvest. Those who grow their own grapes gather relatives and friends and make a festival of handpicking them when they are ripe. When they take a break, the workers will gather for a nice lunch of bread, cheese, and last year's wine before they get back to careful picking. When the grapes are pressed, alcohol and sugar levels are measured to determine the quality of wine that is produced, and if the wine is to be sold, the price will be determined by the quality. Italian wine is not very high in alcohol content, nor is alcoholism a prevalent issue in Italy. Italians actually frown on drunkenness, for it runs contrary to *la bella figura*—the dignified presence with which they are expected to carry themselves. *La vendemmia* is a happy time of the year that brings friends and family together in the *giardino*, garden, to enjoy good flavors, a few laughs, and the spirit of good company.

Winemaking, like the mealtime itself, is another very social way to nourish the body and soul. Italians are not isolated, solitary individuals. They believe that pleasure is magnified when shared with others.

My uncle Beppe, born and raised in Naples, lived to be almost one hundred years old. All of his mental faculties and body

Interessante!
Some of the better-known Italian wines include:
Asti Spumante
a sparkling wine from the Piedmont region of the North
Chianti
a full-bodied red wine from Tuscany
Lambrusco
a lightly sparkling white or red wine from Emilia Romagna
Marsala
a more liqueur-type wine from Sicily

parts were in good working order right through to the end. Not a day went by when he wasn't asked to share his secrets for a long healthy life. He always replied, "A daily glass of wine or two, olive oil instead of butter, a lot of hard work with the hands, and a little bit of time to relax." It sure worked for him!

Make mealtime a social experience.

"*Dai,* Mina, *hai fatto troppo,* you did too much!" Tina was referring to the antipasto, a course normally reserved for holidays.

"*Uffà!*" Mina exclaimed with a wave of her hand. "Go on, today's a celebration."

Tina and Mario had been invited to the Panico home in Salerno for the traditional Sunday *pranzo,* dinner. The air was filled with music and the aroma of fresh pasta sauce. Young Enrico and Marcello pulled two more chairs around the table for their guests of honor, and all eyes widened with delight as their mom presented them with a tray of thinly sliced prosciutto of Parma wrapped around large cold slices of bright orange cantaloupe.

"Mmm, *che buono!*" ten-year-old Marcello cried, drilling a pointer finger into his cheek, a gesture that means "delicious!"

"*Mangia, mangia' che ti fa' bene,*" Mina responded proudly, "eat; it will do you good."

And thus the festivities began at an Italian table one ordinary Sunday afternoon, in a land where the event of breaking bread is anything but ordinary. In fact, eating might be considered one of those everyday triumphs that make life in Italy a continuous series of small celebrations. Sunday dinners are just a bit more formal, though in no way more special than any other day of the week. Typically, relatives, godparents, or family friends are invited, and a few special dishes (meant to make the guests slightly envious) are likely to be served.

No matter what happens throughout the day, a healthful combination of simple Mediterranean foods and close family or friends can heal whatever ails you. As Mina told me once, "If you go to the table feeling down, you leave feeling like you're on top of the world. Your body feels strong and your spirit is uplifted." In Italy, the entire mealtime procedure—from cooking to cleanup—is a microcosm of all that nurtures life. Italians like to sit around the table for hours—especially during holidays—lingering over each course to savor not only the flavors of the food but, above all, the company. Advice from the old to the young is somehow more palatable, too, when given in conjunction with *la buona tavola*, good eating at the dinner table. The dinner table is also therapeutic. The attitude towards emotional distress is, "Who better to put you on the mend than loving family and close friends?" There was nothing we couldn't discuss at the dinner table. All opinions, feelings, and facts were not only welcomed—they were expected. The table was where we went to heal, to celebrate life, and to rejoice in our blessings.

The other day, I was reading about an ancient oriental healing art that involved therapeutic sound. For those of us who are involved in cross-cultural comparisons, it is common to look for universal concepts that hold true for people from most cultures as well as behaviors that seem to be confined to a particular culture. I began to think that using sound as a therapeutic tool is perhaps an instinct that has no cultural boundaries; it seems to be a universally understood concept.

In the U.S., for instance, the sale of table-top water cascades has skyrocketed. Many of us also like to unwind with some soft music when we get home from work. If we feel angry, we might play hard rock to let our frustrations out. If we feel sad, we might put on heart-breaking love ballads that seem to cry along with us. In any case, sound just makes us feel better. Meditators use the sound of their breathing to bring the focus inward. The repetition of the breath lulls one into a meditative state, as does chanting. Lively conversation can likewise swell the soul with joy. To Italians, the sound of voices around the table has its own therapeutic allure.

While the novice listener might interpret it as chaotic clamor, in reality dinnertime in an Italian home is a rather happy blend of auditory stimuli that you can grow quite fond of—from the clinking of dainty new crystal to the clanking of old iron pots. The human vocal element only adds richness to the mix. Animated adult voices raised in anticipation compete with the squeals and whines of children, for whom dinner always comes too slowly. An emotional aria from the kitchen radio makes the ambience complete. Someone ought to record a CD of Italian kitchen and dining room

Interessante!

In 1554, when Hernando Cortez returned to the Old World from Mexico, he brought with him a small, fleshy, yellow sphere-shaped fruit which Italians named the pomo d'oro *(golden apple). In the course of the next two hundred years, thanks to the magical Italian soil, the cherry-like fruits evolved into larger, lusher, ruby-colored tomatoes, much juicier and sweeter than their ancestors. Now the tomato, or* pomodoro, *is a key ingredient in Italian dishes. They may be served stuffed with rice and beans, sliced and alternated with slices of mozzarella for a nice antipasto, or pureed and seasoned for use as tomato sauce over pasta.*

sounds. They warm you from body to soul. Mealtime in Italy is a kaleidoscope of sensations, where sights, smells, sounds, and textures come together to sustain the total person.

For many Italians, the midday meal is the largest, especially in regions where shopkeepers still close and go home for the mid-afternoon dinner and *siesta*, nap. But for others, the supper table is the only time the whole family can gather together, and because of that, it becomes the most important meal of the day. The main mealtime assures at least one block of time when family members stop whatever they are doing to reconvene, talk about their days, argue about politics, joke about their follies, or inform one another about the latest news or gossip. Because the setting is personal and intimate, kids don't usually invite friends or eat at friends' houses during the family's daily mealtime. Company comes occasionally, usually for celebrations.

Start with some basic supplies and simple recipes.
Now that you have an idea of the meaning of the Italian table experience—good food and good conversation—you might be ready to make some subtle changes to your menus to include some nutritious Italian cuisine. If you want to keep basic Mediterranean meal ingredients on hand, your pantry and refrigerator should include the following essential items:

- Dry pasta of various shapes and sizes
- Crusty Italian round bread
- Garlic
- "Flat" Italian parsley
- Extra-virgin olive oil
- Fresh native tomatoes (or canned plum tomatoes)
- Fresh mozzarella
- Fresh basil (when possible)
- Oregano
- Cannelloni beans and chick peas
- Parmesan cheese
- Fresh fruits and vegetables
- Fresh fish

After you have stocked your home with some good Italian staples, it is time to try some simple, basic recipes. The Italian women in my family were a curious lot when it came to sharing recipes. Passing recipes from mother to daughter was the only way to get at the truth, for the daughter got an *in vivo*, live opportunity to see and analyze every ingredient and procedure that went into the preparation. Usually, recipes were not written down, but simply committed to memory. Getting a straightforward recipe from a relative or *paesano*, hometown neighbor, was a different matter altogether. It sometimes took years to figure out an accurate facsimile of the original dish. Every woman in our circle was so proud of their specialties, they would always leave one ingredient out, or report the wrong amount of something, or add an ingredient that had no business being there. Of course *i furbi*, the sneaks, were found out eventually when the recipe was prepared and "something" just didn't taste quite like Aunt Anita's original ricotta cake or Uncle Nick's marinara sauce. So over the years, several variations would be tested, and after consultation with others, at last the original recipe would be deduced by trial and error.

Interessante!

Sagre *is the word for Italy's local summer food festivals, which center principally around fresh produce, such as the Eggplant Fair (Corigliano, August 14), and the Blueberry and Raspberry Fair (Trasaghis-Udine, month of August). Two million Italians participate in the August* sagre, *most of which take place in the south.*

Some of the warmest memories I have of my mother, Rachele, are linked to the love she put into all of her dishes. She loved to cook and bake, and took such pride in the final product that she would practically hold her breath in anticipation of our delighted faces after taking a bite. In *mamma's* lifetime, she collected enough recipes to fill an encyclopedia, and I am lucky enough to have inherited them. They are all in her handwriting, passed down from her mother, aunts, and other Italian *paesani*, and all have been tested at our D'Agostino Italian *tavolo* over the years. Here are just a couple of the "evolved" and original versions of the family favorites that I, too, will pass down to future generations. Just don't forget that food is a celebration to be shared, so gather your loved ones and *mangia*, eat! You deserve to honor your life with good food, good friends, and unhurried living.

SPAGHETTI AND MEATBALLS ALLA MAMMA

This is a great winter dish because it is hearty and can be made with canned tomatoes without sacrificing flavor.

3/4 lb each of ground beef and ground pork

1 egg

1 clove garlic, crushed

5-6 sprigs flat Italian parsley, finely chopped

Pinch salt and pepper

1/2 cup grated cheese

1 cup Italian prepared or fresh bread crumbs

Mix everything together in a large bowl and form into balls of about two inches in diameter. In a skillet, brown the meatballs in hot olive oil, then remove from the pan and drain. Add to the sauce as it simmers (recipe follows) and let them finish cooking.

TOMATO SAUCE

3 tablespoons extra-virgin olive oil
3–4 cloves garlic, chopped
1-28-ounce can plum tomatoes, blended; or 4 pounds fresh plum
  tomatoes, blended
Handful fresh basil, chopped, or 3 tbsp. dried basil
2–3 sprigs parsley, chopped
1/4 cup white or red wine
Salt and pepper to taste.

Heat oil in large saucepan, then add chopped garlic and sauté until lightly golden. Add tomatoes, basil, wine, and salt and pepper. Simmer for one-half hour. Then add meatballs and let simmer another half-hour. When done, remove meatballs to be eaten to the side, and pour sauce over one pound of spaghetti, cooked *al dente* (until just tender, but not soft).

MOM'S PESTO

Summer is the best time to enjoy the fresh flavors of the garden, in which most Italians will at least grow the basics: tomatoes, basil, parsley, mint, and zucchini. No cooking is required for this delightfully healthful dish.

2 large juicy ripe tomatoes
2–3 handfuls of fresh basil leaves
5–6 cloves of garlic
Salt and pepper to taste
1/2 cup extra-virgin olive oil
2 tablespoons pine nuts (optional)
Parmesan cheese to garnish

Mix all ingredients, except for cheese, in a blender and puree. Pour over fresh, hot spaghetti or your favorite pasta shape that is cooked *al dente*, and top with grated Parmesan cheese.

The Occasional Italian Dessert
MAMMA'S OWN BISCOTTI

Biscotti and Anginettes are two Italian cookies that are slightly sweet and make a wonderful ending to special meals. Here are the keepsakes from Mom's treasured recipe collection. Please note that baking is one of the rare times butter is used in southern Italian cuisine, though you may substitute olive oil if you wish.

1-1/2 sticks butter, softened

3 eggs

1-1/4 cup sugar

1 teaspoon vanilla extract

1 teaspoon almond extract

3 cups flour

3 teaspoon baking powder

1 cup chopped walnuts

Cream the butter and sugar together until fluffy. Add eggs and extracts. Beat well. In another bowl, mix the dry ingredients together, then add to the butter mixture, blending well. Shape into three long rectangular loaves and place on a greased cookie sheet. Bake in a 350° oven for about twenty-five minutes, or until golden brown. When slightly cool, you may glaze the biscotti if desired, (recipe follows) and slice the loaves at a gentle angle and bake in the oven for five minutes more to harden. These cookies are great dunked in coffee!

BISCOTTI GLAZE

1/2 cup confectioners sugar

1 teaspoon almond extract

3 tablespoons milk

Mix all ingredients together and drizzle on warm biscotti loaves.

RACHELE'S ANGINETTES

2 sticks butter
1/2 cup sugar
2 eggs
1 teaspoon vanilla
1/2 cup fresh orange juice
3 teaspoons baking powder
1/2 teaspoon baking soda
3 cups flour

Cream the sugar and butter together until fluffy, then add eggs, orange juice, and vanilla.

In a separate bowl, stir dry ingredients together, then add to the butter mixture and blend well. Drop by teaspoons onto lightly greased pan and bake in a 350°F oven for 10–12 minutes. When cool, use the recipe below to frost.

ANGINETTE FROSTING

1/2 stick butter, softened
3/4 box confectioners sugar
2 tablespoons orange juice
2–3 tablespoons milk (enough to give icing a creamy consistency)

Mix all ingredients until creamy. Smoothe over cooled anginettes.

chapter five

WExalth that Goes *Beyond Money*

*All the energy Americans devote to the accumulation and manage-
ment of money, the hours spent thinking about how to amass it,
organize it, invest it, will it, spend it, keep it, share it or not share it.
Romans instead devote their energy to other things—to looking well,
eating well, loving well, and spending time with their families.*

—ALAN EPSTEIN, *AS THE ROMANS DO*

Italian society is an ancient culture that has continually corrected itself
throughout the course of its evolution. An inquisitive glance in Italy's
direction gives us important clues as to what works and what doesn't.
The elements that foster *la dolce vita* have remained invariant throughout the centuries. One of these elements is the Italian perspective on
wealth. At an early age, I learned the Italian angle on money, work,
and what it really means to be rich from an Italian perspective. My
Italian family taught me these six important lessons about financial
and personal wealth:

1. Work is a privilege, so work hard and do your job well.
2. What you save is more important than what you make.
3. Share your good fortune with those who need it—family first,
   then others.
4. Respect and take care of the things you have, and don't waste.

5. Don't worry about what the next guy has.
6. Think of wealth as more than just money.

Work is a privilege, so work hard and do your job well.

My grandfather Domenico used to say he was the wealthiest man on the planet. "I have three million dollars," he would say, "Rachele, Saverio, and Rosario," his three children. Pop came to America at the turn of the century, with barely a lira in his pocket. His goal was to survive the devastating poverty of his hometown and be able to send money back to his mother and the other relatives who remained behind. He did all that and more. In the U.S., he became a model citizen. He was grateful to his new country and worked night and day to learn a trade and earn enough money to provide for his family, both here and in Italy. Pop apprenticed with an elderly cobbler, worked hard, and eventually bought his own shoe shop, to which he dedicated himself every day for the rest of his life. Some believed that my grandfather was born to be a cobbler, that he must have had a natural talent for it or had discovered his true calling in life. None of that could be farther from the truth. He simply believed with all his heart that work was a privilege and that whatever life hands you to do, you might as well do it the very best way you can. In a different place and time, perhaps Pop would have been a singer. He sang everywhere he went, all of the time. He loved getting up at parties and belting out a good aria. However, Domenico ultimately believed people could make themselves happy with any cards they were dealt. He believed that honest work deserves to be respected, and when you give it your best, the rewards will come. Training yourself to think like this may not be easy at first, but it becomes easier the more you practice.

Let's face it. Most of us don't have dream jobs. We may have a job we like well enough, or in some cases don't like at all. However, seeing our work in a positive light fosters feelings of satisfaction and happiness, no matter what the particulars of the job or what kind of work we do. My friend Marco, for example, lives in Naples. He is so passionate about his art, that it is all he talks about with whomever will listen. His unique style is to blend computer images with traditional oil on canvas. Every weekend he is requested to give an art show in one part of Italy or another. He has a very loyal following, but he is not only known as an artist—Marco is also a dedicated pediatrician! If you listen to him talk, it is quite clear which of the two occupations makes every cell of his body come alive. That is not to say he neglects his medical practice in the least—quite the contrary. He dedicates the entire week to taking care of his patients and staying current with medical research. To watch him work, you would think that he, like my grandfather, was meant to be a doctor. Instead, he will tell you that he was meant to do the work that supports him and his family.

Even if you don't have your ideal job, there is a way you can immediately feel better about doing the work you do. Domenico and Marco's *dolce vita* perspectives on work enabled them to:

❦ Emphasize the advantages of their full time jobs
❦ Minimize the negatives of their jobs
❦ Stay involved with their hearts' true desires outside of their regular jobs

Emphasize the advantages of your work.

Pop always emphasized what he loved about the shoe business. He knew nothing at all about shoes before he came to the United States. In fact, there were times when he didn't even own a pair of shoes. His favorite proverb—which he often repeated when we complained about something—was, "I felt sorry for myself for having no shoes, until I saw someone who had no feet." That will give you an idea of how he approached work. He looked for all of the positives he could find because some people had no work at all. Making and selling shoes gave Domenico the means to provide shoes to people who might not have otherwise been able to afford shoes. He found ways to keep his prices low and make a living at the same time.

Owning a shoe store provided my grandfather with a way to help his community, a way of giving thanks for being able to live and work in America. That, to him, was a real advantage. He could make sure that all of the neighborhood children had slippers, whether they could afford them or not. He often bought slippers from the wholesaler and gave them away—instead of selling them—to mothers who told him their children were going barefoot around the house. His customers considered him family. Dom became a hero of the neighborhood.

Besides reminding yourself of the advantages to your present work, there is one other thing that helped Pop grow to love his work—he absorbed himself in it, minute by minute. As he sat on his cobbler's bench, replacing the neighborhood's soles and heels, every shoe took on the personality of the person who wore it. As a finishing touch, he polished them to a sparkle at no extra charge. Happiness researcher Mihaly Csikszentmihalyi called "flow" the process of being totally and joyfully engaged in the activity at hand. Pop never kept his eye on the clock to see when his work hours were up. He took a micro-approach to his tasks—each subtask, like nailing a heel, gluing a sole, stitching a trim—became a source of satisfaction to him. Pop liked to lose himself in the process of his work with an unassuming engagement. Whether one is a painter, doctor, garbage collector, or shoemaker, my grandfather believed that the only real disgrace is wasting your time by not putting in your best effort. When you are fully absorbed in the details of your work, time becomes more joyful and almost undetectable.

Today, try listing all of the advantages of your current job. List the obvious direct advantages first—for example, your weekly paycheck—as well as the not-so-obvious, indirect advantages—such as the good feeling you get when your coworkers give you a compliment. When you are at work tomorrow, be conscious of giving your complete attention to the mechanics of each task you perform. Engage your mind and attention completely as you carry out your assignments. Try to improve on or find new ways of doing old tasks. For example, figure out some new ways to describe and explain the next car you sell, or discover a new function on your word processor that will make your typed report even more outstanding. You will find that as you make the extra effort to put new touches on everything you do throughout your workday, your sense of satisfaction and happiness will steadily grow.

Minimize the negatives of your work.
There will always be aspects of work that seem tedious, stressful, or unpleasant, even if you have a job that you generally enjoy. The prob-

lem is that once you focus on these negativities, they take on a disproportionate life of their own. Any negative aspect of work that you dwell on will eventually overpower its positive aspects. From time to time we all have to deal with the coworker from hell, the monotony of doing grunt work, or the staff meeting where we couldn't get a word in edgewise. We all know the feeling of giving a presentation that flops or trying to appease a customer only to get the phone slammed in our ear. Some of us know what it feels like to be up for a raise or promotion, only to get told that budget cuts preclude any pay increases in the near future. What can we do to deflate the power of these work-related negativities? First, list the negative points, one by one. Next, put them into perspective by performing a reality check. Have you exaggerated the negativity? Can you come up with evidence to indicate the situation is not quite as bleak as you have perceived it? Finally, figure out what you can do to turn this negative aspect of work into a positive. Here is an example.

Write out the negativity: "It doesn't seem like I'll ever get a raise."

Reality check: "Just because I didn't get a raise this year doesn't automatically mean that I won't get one next year. That is an illogical assumption."

Turning negative into positive: "This year I will concentrate on doing things that will add credibility to my request for a raise. I will also make a point of enjoying the present positive aspects of my job more. Instead of focusing on next year's job evaluation, I will serenely enjoy the daily aspects of my job one day at a time and try to improve on everything I do."

Stay involved with your heart's true desire.
While Domenico managed to make a make a respectable living, his family and his singing were his true heart's desire, and despite the long hours it took to run his own business, he always made it a point to make time for both.

There is a lot of well-meaning advice that says if we stick to our heart's desire we can eventually make a living at it. This may be true or it may not be, but the reality is that most of us cannot spend several years waiting to make a living writing, drawing, or trying to develop a private practice in Eastern meditation—especially if we have families to support! That doesn't mean we have to abandon what we love to do! I once knew someone who longed to be a pianist. Gracie spent several years trying to make it, but finally realized she was not of concert caliber, and that jobs in the field were few and far between. Facing this fact was so painful for her that she gave up the piano entirely to study architecture—her second love. However, even as her career as an architect blossomed, there was emptiness inside of her because by erasing the piano from her life completely (e.g., "If I can't do what I love all the time, I won't do it at all"), she was denying an integral part of herself. Once she realized what was happening, she began to spend a little time each evening getting reacquainted with her old love by brushing up on her old music lessons. Not only has her work as an architect taken on a happier dimension, but now her life in general is much more fulfilling.

What you save is more important than what you make.
Money experts confirm what my grandparents taught us years ago—that the size of one's income is less important than how well we handle

the money we earn. Most people become millionaires not because of how much money they made over their lifetime, but because of how relatively little they spent.

Italians are still attentive spenders today—just as they were in my grandparents' time. Salaries are not as high as they would be in the U.S., yet the cost of living in many parts of Italy is relatively equal to ours. Italians are among Europe's greatest savers, often putting away up to 20 percent of their earnings. That doesn't mean they are miserly, but it does mean that they buy less and they shop for quality. Italians don't accumulate a lot of goods, but instead take good care of their things so they will last.

How do Italians resist the temptation to spend more than they have? Through the principle of *non esagerare*, nothing in excess! They are apprehensive about going overboard when it comes to spending, stockpiling, or doing anything to excess. Beyond needing money for our basic human needs, there are probably some extras we can eliminate from our lives and not miss at all. Perhaps we can get away with two pairs of black shoes and resist buying a third. Instead of going out to dinner twice a week, we can cut back to once. Maybe we can bring our briefcases to a repair shop to get those tears stitched instead of throwing them away prematurely. Italians resist becoming a society of disposables. The money saved from making small changes can eventually become investments that will yield interest.

Psychologist David Myers points out that there is only a modest correlation between well-being and being well-off. After a certain point, having more money does not ensure greater happiness. The Roman stoic Seneca, who was extremely altruistic with his own wealth, believed that anything beyond what takes care of one's needs is excess. There is a point of diminishing returns when it comes to material acquisitions. Italians know that. Their approach to wealth includes cautious spending, choosing quality over quantity, saving more than one spends, and adopting a holistic approach to wealth—which includes making time to appreciate other pleasures in life, too.

Interestingly, money experts today are no longer touting the necessity of higher academic degrees and more frequent promotions in order to achieve financial health. After a certain point, additional academic degrees may no longer be cost-effective if they leave us with large loans to pay back and not enough career opportunities or time to catch up. I learned two powerful financial secrets from my Italian heritage:

1. Make a commitment to put away a certain amount of money from each paycheck; and
2. Focus on enjoying what you already have.

Think of some activities that make you feel rich without having to empty your wallet to do them. Do you enjoy having a cup of coffee with friends at the local bookshop? What about playing hooky from work one afternoon to take a hike in the woods? Instead of having to make big expensive vacation plans, how about taking your family to local state attractions you haven't had time to explore before?

In addition to focusing on enjoying what you already have, decide how much you will take from your paycheck each week to put into your savings. Write that figure down—and stick to it. Perhaps you are just making ends meet now, and can't imagine being able to put anything away. If that is the case, don't despair. Simply think of what extras you can cut down on and devote that money to your savings. Keep a jar into which you put the change you would have spent on that extra can of soda or that candy bar. Your health as well as your peace of mind will benefit, and before long, even those stray quarters and one-dollar bills will add up!

Matteo Pennachi is an example of how one can feel rich without having a lot of money. This Roman made the *Guinness Book of World Records* by traveling around the world without a lira in his pocket. His travels took him across two oceans, a dozen countries and two continents, all the while relying on the goodness of humankind to get him through. He claims he wanted to get by because of who he was, not how much money he had. Instead of focusing on traveling first-class, he focused on the joy of seeing new lands, meeting new people, and enriching his soul independently of money.

Share your good fortune with those who need it— family first, then others.

My Italian family always believed that no matter how much or how little you have, sharing is one way to feel rich. Generosity is the rule rather than the exception. Many years ago, I traveled to a very small, rural town outside of Benevento, basically in the middle of nowhere, to visit relatives. It was truly the land that time had forgotten, and despite my grandmother's generosity throughout the years in sending money back home, these wonderful human beings still lived with very few modern-day amenities or material possessions. Their lives consisted of working hard in the fields from early morning until dark. When I came to visit, they took out their best wine, made homemade cakes, and sat around me at the table in true celebratory style. What they had—or didn't have—wasn't an issue. They offered me their beds to sleep in, their bathroom to wash up in, and their unconditional love and acceptance—which no amount of money in the world could buy. Although it was clear that my cousins had very little, I felt as if I was among the wealthiest people on earth. By the time I was ready to leave the "old country," I understood a little better what true wealth meant.

We all fall into periods of self-centeredness now and then. At times we may even forget how exhilarating it feels to share who we are and what we have with others. True generosity includes more than just sharing money, but also sharing talents, time, our ability to listen, or our capacity to run errands or baby-sit someone else's kids. The different kinds of wealth we can share are endless. Try listing all of the qualities you might have to offer others, and you will see what I mean. Altruistic behavior is commonplace in Italy. Volunteering at church or at the kids' school is another way Italians frequently share their wealth. If you would like to see how good donating a bit of your time can feel, all you need to do is pick up the phone and pledge an hour or two helping in a convalescent hospital or tutoring students at your local school who need extra help.

Respect and take care of the things you have, and don't waste.

In Grandma Angela's house, nothing went to waste. She disdained extravagances and buying possessions as status symbols. If something was still in working order, it was unthinkable to replace it just to have a newer

Interessante!

Balance and avoiding excess promote psychological wealth. Mihaly Csikszentmihaly believes that all good things in life—food, sex, relaxation, etc.—promote happiness in their proper doses, but the effect is not additive—there is definitely a point of diminishing returns.

model. When we ate at her house and didn't use our paper napkins, those napkins would be folded and saved for the next time. If she could clean up a spill with only half of a paper towel, the other half would be torn off and saved in a drawer. Even loose pennies had a dignified place alongside the dollar bills in the money drawer. Money was money, and no matter if you had a good or bad week in terms of earnings, you still put aside as much as you could for a rainy day.

Nonna Angela taught me that buying too many things is like taking your money and throwing it in the wastebasket. "Cluttering your house with possessions only clutters your mind," she would say. It leads to confusion and disorganization. Sometimes we even buy duplicates of something we already have because the originals were buried under clutter and we have forgotten about them!

I once helped a friend clean out her kitchen and as I went through the baking cabinets I pulled out thirteen little bottles of candy sprinkles. Thirteen! Some were opened, some were still sealed, some were tucked away in the back and forgotten. The most recent bottles had price labels that said $2.99. Multiply that by thirteen and you'll get an idea of what a nice little sum could have been earning interest.

Don't worry about what the next guy has.

My grandparents lived modestly. They had a modest house, a modest car, and modest furnishings—but in return, they were tranquil in knowing there was money in the bank for a rainy day, and that they owed money to no one. They paid no attention to what friends and neighbors had. Of course, in the old days, there were no such things as credit cards, but even when they did come into vogue, no one in my house wanted one. Italians prefer to buy things they can pay cash for, and if they do use a credit card, they tend to pay it off in full each month, since it is wasteful to throw hard-earned money away on interest.

We could probably all benefit by buying a lot less than we currently do. It is human nature to want to buy things other people have, like that nice new luxury car or that beautiful designer suit. Sometimes we feel less valid if we don't have as much as our neighbors. It is important to remember, however, that living debt-free and driving a ten-year-old Chevy can give much more peace of mind than having to figure out how you will manage to make the next payment for the BMW! It is not hard to realize that wanting things we don't need or can't have creates unhappiness.

Your mental attitude is what determines your moods. Fortunately, we can purposefully create an attitude that fosters happiness. Moods don't just fall from the sky. Feelings are a reaction to our voluntary thoughts and perceptions of the world around us. In the car example above, for instance, we can choose to focus on the positive aspects of driving that older car—for example, being free of debt, getting our money's worth from the vehicle, and so forth—or we can focus on how upset we are about not driving a luxury car.

Which perspective makes a person feel better? The answer is obvious!

My grandparents believed that envy invites bad luck. In lieu of wasting energy complaining about things we didn't have, they taught us to devote some time reflecting on what we did have. If you want to live peacefully and happily, their technique really works! With a little effort you can train yourself to see the glass as half-full and let the little joys take primary focus. How is this done? By giving ourselves a good argument whenever we feel negative or envious of things others have. It is helpful to write negative feelings down on paper, and then refute them with contradictory evidence. For example, let's say you just found out that a friend of yours is making twice as much money as you make. You feel jealous and begin to put yourself down for not having made the same career choices your friend made so that you, too, could be earning what she is. This way of thinking will depress you every time. Instead, refute the underlying assumption. Why should you have made the same career choices that your friend made? How can you feel better about the choices that you did make? Did they fit in better with your needs at the time? Is your job better suited to you than hers would be, despite the money? Ask yourself to come up with evidence to refute your jealous feelings. Then, in this example, if money is a real issue, try coming up with some action-oriented ideas to increase your earnings or make some extra money on the side. Action works. Brooding only leads to the blues!

Think of wealth as more than just money.

Sometimes, in concentrating on the balance sheet of our bank accounts, we can forget how wealthy we really are! Here are four *dolce vita* suggestions for feeling like an instant millionaire, no matter what your financial portfolio looks like:

1. Strive for a balance in your life.
2. Take stock of the possessions that mean something to you.
3. Polish and care for the possessions you have.
4. Do more work in less time.

Strive for balance.

"When you attain a balance in your life," said Luisa from Trieste, "you will feel wealthy." Achieving a balanced life means paying attention to all the aspects of your life that enrich you. We can make ourselves feel rich by distributing our focus among achievements at work, spirituality, culture, social life, family life, physical health, and leisure time. Here is how:

Try drawing a large circle, and then divide it in a pie chart fashion, making each wedge, or area of your life, proportionate to the time you devote to it. Next, draw another large circle below it, divided into the same number of sections, only this time the sections will be proportionate to the amount of time you would like to spend on each of the areas that are important to your life. Now you can start to think of ways to schedule your time to be more in line with the "ideal" pie chart. Also, from your pie chart diagrams, you can clearly see that there is much more to life than money and work.

Most Italians will tell you they work to live, and not the other way around. They refuse to work endless hours at the expense of life's other treasures. One of these treasures is evident by the culture's devotion to the arts. The arts are considered to be treasures of the Italian soul. Music, painting, theatre, opera, dance, and architecture provide aesthetic beauty that we often let slide when life gets busy. Taking time for the arts renews the spirit, as will a good game of *scopa* (a card game) with friends, or a stimulating argument about politics or religion. Love and passion are also high on the list of what Italians refer to as *le piccole grandi cose della vita*, the small yet great things in life.

When our lives are out of balance, certain sections of our life pie chart get narrow or disappear. When you see that happening, take it as your cue to start scheduling in more time for the neglected areas that make life worth living to you. I recently flipped through a popular financial magazine and read that while Americans now have more money than ever, they complain about not having the time to enjoy it! When asked what they would buy if they could buy anything they wanted, most answered, "More free time." Think about what areas of your life are important to you, and then take action by distributing your time among them. You will notice a difference almost right away in your level of well-being.

Take stock of your possessions.

I don't believe people who tell me money isn't important. Money is important, but as my friend Stefania once said, "Up to a certain point, money allows you to live in a dignified way. It is nice to have money for the things you need and want, but beyond that, what's the point of obsessing over having more and more? Better to relax and enjoy what you have." Learning to enjoy what you already have is much easier if you do this simple exercise. Take an inventory of your current possessions, and try to put a general monetary value on them. Some of your things will have a sentimental value that money could never buy. For those items, think of what price you might put on that object if you absolutely had no choice but to sell it. For example, I have a picture of my mother, who recently passed away. I would not sell that picture for any money in the world. Since I know no one but myself would care so much about it, I might feel safe giving it a price of one billion dollars. That way, I would be sure no one would try to buy it.

From the Italian perspective, some things are just not for sale. The family home is the most obvious example. Home is where the family is nurtured, and, when possible, the family home usually gets passed down through the generations. Not only do Italians refuse to sell their homes, but also the older generations even refuse to leave their homes—unless someone they trust will house-sit! Getting Grandma Angela to come to our house for dinner for even just one holiday was a prime example.

"But who will watch the house?" she would say, with a voice that dared anyone to argue with that.

It wasn't so much that the house was in real danger of being vandalized as it was that leaving it unguarded was like inviting trouble and disrespecting what one has been given. An Italian home is the extension of the family that dwells within its walls. It is a focal point of stability, grounding, good feelings, and pride. You could have offered my grandmother suitcases full of large-note bills, and she still would never sell her house in a million years.

Care for the things you have.

Italians like nice things, but they don't necessarily have to be new. My friend Paolo from Ancona drives a twelve-year-old Audi that you couldn't pry away from him with a crowbar. Like Grandma's house, it is not for sale. He wipes it clean every morning before he takes it out for a ride, and re-polishes any minor scratches each day. The inside is just as pristine; in fact, it looks brand new. The desire to make a good impression, *la bella figura*, accounts for only a small part of the Italian attachment to the things they have. Paolo once said, "I have driven many places in this car. I have had many wonderful experiences. It has taken me wherever I needed to go, so I take good care of it, too." The old Audi made Paolo feel wealthy—psychologically—especially when it sparkled like new. You could have offered him a new BMW and he would still choose his twelve-year-old car—obviously it had become an extension of himself!

When we take care of the things we buy, we save money and buy less. Make a list of things you would like to salvage and restore—things that mean something to you, but you thought needed to be thrown away. Then tackle one such project a week until you have gone down the list.

Do more work in less time.

One of the things we all wish we could have more of is free time. A very effective way that my Italian colleagues get around this issue is by focusing intensely and exclusively on the project at hand. It is amazing how much time we waste while working due to distractions. Often we are not aware of how many times we get up to get a drink of water or go to the restroom while in the middle of working on something. Then, before you know it, we meet a colleague along the way, start chatting, and by the time we get back to what we were doing, twenty or so minutes have already slipped by. Then it takes another five or ten minutes to regather our thoughts!

We can train our inner power of focus by devoting specific chunks of time to each project we tackle. This could include tasks at home or at work. Start out by allowing for small segments of time, during which you promise yourself that nothing will steal your attention. Perhaps you can work for twenty-minute segments this week, and increase to thirty minutes next week, until you are working for segments of an hour and a half at a time. In between those set intervals, give your brain—and body—a good five- or ten-minute stretch, but then get back to work promptly for the next interval. Focusing means not letting anything come between you and your project—neither your own thoughts, nor the interruption of others. Thus you can take the phone off the hook, or let it roll over to the answering machine. If others interrupt you while your are at your desk, tell them you will get back to them as soon as you have finished what you have in front of you. Tell them you do not want to lose your train of thought. Most people will understand, as long as you keep your promise to get back to them. When you begin to do your work with focus, you will feel strong and competent like never before. The reward you will reap in the end is more free time to distribute among your pie chart of life-balancing activities. Free time adds to personal wealth and it doesn't cost a thing! Start thinking of some wonderful ways you can spend your newfound free time.

chapter six

Putting Your
Best Foot Forward

The culture loves beauty, depends on beauty,
is addicted to beauty. The single word to describe
all good things, whether they mean great, terrific wonderful,
marvelous, fantastic, satisfying, or well done, is bello.

—ALAN EPSTEIN, *AS THE ROMANS DO*

To Italians, presenting yourself well in thought, word, and deed is a matter of personal dignity. *Fare la bella figura*—literally making a good figure—alludes to the idea of putting your best foot forward. The foreign visitor to Italy is typically amazed to observe how polished the men and women of the *bel paese* look, how good they appear to feel about themselves, and how graciously they interact with one another. Italian life is undeniably lived with a constant eye toward aesthetic beauty, dignity, and civility. Learning to enhance the body and mind one is born with is more important than having been endowed with genetic perfection.

Whether practicing *la bella figura* leads to well-being, or well-being leads to making a good impression, the end result is the same. If you are happy on the inside, it shows! In fact, research shows that even when you don't feel so bubbly inside, just *acting* happy eventually creates an internal change in that direction. Why? Behaviors change thoughts, and thoughts change behaviors. It doesn't matter which comes first; either one pulls the other in its direction. Thus, if you are not feeling good about yourself on a particular day, try dressing nicely, walking with grace, and smiling. You will notice immediate changes in your feelings. Physically going through the motions will elevate your spirits. Essentially, positive body language promotes positive thoughts and elevates one's self-esteem.

Age has nothing to do with *la bella figura;* however, the way you feel about yourself does. Italian mothers prime their young to cultivate *la bella figura* practically from birth, when they are taught manners and dressed with an aesthetic eye, regardless of convenience. This philosophy continues throughout the life cycle. Professor Marino Di Giovanni is a good example of *la bella figura* in later life. Now in his mid-sixties, his female students still think of him as one of the sexiest professors in Florence. When he walks into the lecture hall, they blush, giggle, and whisper to each other. Judging from the slight smile at the corners of his lips, he is well aware of his prowess. Di Giovanni walks tall and sports a longish silver mane. As he leans over the lectern he projects his voice confidently in a dramatic whisper, "Might perception be simply a cousin to illusion?"

Impatient hands immediately dart up, each trying to be the tallest, the most conspicuous, the worthiest of intellectual exchange. The good professor's self-assured demeanor inspires this kind of magic, and before long the ambience of the entire lecture hall is electrifying. The *bella figura* bestows benefits on both actor and recipient.

If you are wondering how to acquire a sense of *la bella figura* in your everyday life, it is important to understand the three basic components of this concept. *Bella figura* is a **physical**, **behavioral**, and **mental** process.

Acquiring the Physical Bella Figura

The *bella figura* is not a neurotic obsession with looks, but rather an automatic daily protocol for living an upbeat life. Italians don't obsess about their physical appearances, but they do enjoy looking good and experiencing a positive self-image. Psychological findings support the notion that physical appearance *is* related to psychological well-being—for more reasons than first meet the eye. In societies that value physical beauty, it is not surprising that attractive people—those with nice hair, handsome bodies, and symmetrical facial features—are likely to be viewed more favorably by prospective mates, employers, teachers, and acquaintances. This is especially true of first impressions; but of course once we get to know others, often a great personality makes people seem more attractive than they appeared to be at first glance. Fortunately for those of us who weren't blessed with model looks, there's no need to throw in the towel! In Italy, beauty is experienced more from a personal than social perspective. In other words, making yourself feel good first is what counts. *Bella figura* beauty requires only that we learn to appreciate what we have and emphasize our best features. The impact that a good physical presentation has on your social life is second only to the way it makes you feel beautiful inside.

Trying to perfect yourself for the opposite sex may be an exercise in futility, anyway. The research on male-female attraction tells us that, in reality, neither males nor females find physical perfection to be a turn-on in the opposite sex. Rather, it is that slightly tousled hair, or that imperceptibly loosened necktie, that attracts us to someone because we perceive that person to be more human, and thus more like ourselves.

Some simple tips to a physical *bella figura* include the following: a good **skin care** routine, choosing **fashions** that complement your body, keeping yourself **well-groomed**, and staying in strong **physical shape**. Taking good care of yourself and your appearance will boost your self-confidence and help you carry yourself with that classic Italian elegance.

Skin care, Italian-style

In Italy, good skin care is imperative. My grandmother's olive Sicilian complexion literally glowed with health. She used very little make-up—perhaps a little lipstick and rouge—but more importantly, she always washed her face meticulously, and then moisturized it with one or two drops of olive oil. Italy today leads the world in innovative skin-care products. You can't pick up an Italian magazine without seeing glossy ads for the latest wrinkle-busting and firming eye creams—all testimony to the Italian emphasis on good skin care. And yes—old-fashioned olive oil is coming back on the beauty scene in the U.S., too, in a much more sophisticated—and expensive—formulation! Men and women can also make a wonderful exfoliating wash at home, by mixing a bit of sugar with enough olive oil to make a paste. Gently rub this mixture onto your face—or anywhere on your body you want to soften up—and leave it on for thirty minutes before rinsing it off with a very warm washcloth. Your skin will feel baby soft!

Italian women choose the natural look in makeup. They keep the basics on hand, including an eyelash curler, a gentle high-quality mascara, and a neutral matching blush and lipstick—you can even use a lipstick as your blush and save some money. A good smoky eye pencil can be smudged for day or left defined for evening.

Fashion, Italian-style.
Italy is known as the fashion leader of the world, generating innovative and classic styles from the runways of Milan. Grandma Giuseppina was the best-dressed woman in our neighborhood. "Oh, what an elegant woman your grandmother is!" people would say to me. My mother also inherited her sense of fashion and flair. I remember the two women having their hats custom-made and searching for colored cotton or silk gloves to match their dresses and high heels. Grandma was not a wealthy woman, but she considered dressing well to be a necessity. When Italians shop for clothing and accessories, they think quality—not quantity. A few good classic pieces that can be upgraded with new accessories every year will give you the most for your dollar—especially if you shop off-season.

One philosophy my grandfather and I shared was the importance of wearing one's "Sunday best" to work each day. He always wore a neatly pressed shirt and necktie to work in his shoe shop, and I always wore a suit to teach in the university. I daresay neither of our attire was typical for our professions! *Non voglio fare una brutta figura,* Pop would say, I don't want to make a bad impression. We both knew it was about more than just the dress—it was about respect for ourselves and our work.

To follow the fashion protocol of *la bella figura,* a great place to start is your closet. Clear out items that are faddish and outdated; items that have become too small or stretched out; or items you haven't worn in more than a year. Cluttered closets often reflect cluttered minds. Give unused items to charity. Then buy some basic, good quality wardrobe items that are not likely to go out of style, in a color that can be easily accessorized. A black knee-length skirt and some classic black slacks are two examples. They can be worn with any kind of top, sweater, or jacket and will look great year after year if you purchase quality. Italians buy clothes that are built to last. On a lighter note, cellular phones and designer sunglasses are also "must-have" fashion accessories that lend a bit of fun and presence to the Italian *bella figura.*

Grooming

Italians spend a considerable amount of time on meticulous grooming. Pulling your look together by paying attention to detail and hygiene gives the world a signal that you respect and like who you are. That is a very magnetic quality! While perfection isn't the goal, there is a lot we can do to take care of the little things that give us a polished, confident look. For instance, check your nails each night to see if they are chipped or cracked or need a fresh coat of polish. Make sure your shoes are kept shined and in good repair. Perhaps your clothes need pressing, or your suits have become a little frayed around the hems. These are small things that often go unattended to in the bustle of everyday life. Italian men and women place a lot of emphasis on clean, well-groomed hair. Keep your hair regularly trimmed and have fun experimenting with different styles, highlights, lowlights, hennas, or perms.

Getting into Shape, Italian-style

While the *palestra*, gym, is growing in popularity among Italy's youth, the majority of Italians don't rely on heart-stopping aerobic routines to maintain their svelte figures and physiques. Their secret? In addition to eating clean, simple foods, as in the Mediterranean diet, walking and bicycling are part of daily life in the boot-shaped peninsula. From the very young to the very old, people get out regularly into the fresh air and move their bodies. If you want to exercise in the true *dolce vita* tradition, think of exercise as a lifestyle activity as opposed to a concentrated hour of pre-programmed torture! How can you go about this? Figure out what activity you enjoy doing, and do it often! Take long walks, short walks, bike rides to the store, pull weeds often in your garden—do everything you can to keep your body in natural motion throughout the day. You will not only burn more calories this way, but when you are busy, you tend to eat less, too!

The Behaviors of Bella Figura

The second component of *la bella figura* involves **body language** and **social interactions**. These two aspects of behavior are essential for feeling good about ourselves, as well as making a good impression on others. Positive interactions transmit warmth, acceptance, and good feelings, which make people enjoy being around those who practice *la bella figura*.

Body Language

Have you ever caught your reflection in a store window and cringed at what you saw? Perhaps you were slouched over or had a scowl on your face. A cheerful facial expression and confident body posture really have a delightful effect on your state of mind and those around you. Self-confidence is the most attractive quality human beings have the power to communicate. A friend of mine recently told me how her confident body language led her to meet her future husband on the trail where she normally goes hiking: "He said he liked the confident way that I walked, and asked if he could join me! That was just the beginning!"

Kinesics is the study of communication through body movement, posture, gestures, and facial expressions. Essentially it refers to body language. Naturally, there are cultural variations in body language. Italy, for example, enjoys more open flirtation than would be acceptable here, and there is also a more frequent use of gestures. Some body language, however, is universal. Smiling, for instance, indicates friendliness in most cultures. Leaning slightly toward a person as they speak tells them you are interested in what they have to say. Italians love to express themselves openly and transmit their joy for life through facial expressions and confident body movements. Because gesturing is a common form of communication in many parts of Italy, most Italians have become astute observers of body language and facial expressions. One of my Italian colleagues said he could gauge the sincerity of political candidates based on the discrepancy between their words and facial expressions as they gave a public address. Often we are not aware of what our faces are doing as we communicate, but both body posture and facial expression are worth examining in front of a mirror every once in a while. The goal is to make your movements positive and graceful. Also, try to make your facial expressions reflect positive qualities, like joyfulness, kindness, and lovingness. Let your facial expression reflect what you're saying. See that you walk, sit, and move in a way that communicates dignity and confidence. This kind of body language will draw people toward you like a magnet. Make the following exercise a daily routine until you have acquired the confidence you deserve.

Find a regular time each day when you can have a few minutes to yourself (to avoid any self-consciousness). Ten minutes will do. Stand in front of a full-length mirror and imagine that you are talking to someone who typically makes you feel uncomfortable or self-conscious. Try reenacting a recent dialogue you had which didn't turn out as you would have liked it to. At first, this may be awkward, but if you role-play like this a few times, your confidence will snowball and you will automatically learn to handle any situation with poise.

Another good way to develop confident body language is to imitate others who already display it. According to social cognitive psychologist Albert Bandura, the sole act of observing and imitating someone helps us learn those behaviors ourselves. Watch how confident people speak and move. If you don't know anyone who fits that description, observe different actors on TV. Imagine yourself in their shoes throughout the day and you will eventually begin to incorporate the desired behavior automatically into your own repertoire.

Social Interactions

In addition to confident posture and positive facial expressions, the way we interact with others directly affects the impression we make on them. Simple traits like courtesy, manners, and basic pleasant demeanor go a long way in making a good impression.

Long after they invented eating utensils, Italians continue to be meticulous about table manners and protocol. Once I joined a business colleague for a *bistecca alla fiorentina*, a typical Florentine grilled steak. We took his navy sports convertible from the main business district in Florence up through the winding narrow hillside roads that led to a chic elevated part of town called Fiesole. Roberto removed his jacket and gave it to the *cameriere*, waiter, who was a longtime acquaintance of his by now, and indicated that he'd like a table *al fuori*, outdoors. We were promptly shown to our table and lavished with attention as the waiter handed us a menu.

"Non e' necessario," Roberto said with a confident wave of the hand. "We already know what we'll have." He gave his order using the familiar *tu* form of address as is the protocol between client and waiter, and the waiter naturally returned with the more formal *lei*.

Politeness and good manners are essential to Italian social behavior. Roberto used his silverware artfully and knew exactly how to gently position them at the top of his plate upon finishing the meal. His elegant table demeanor was part of the never-ending *spettacolo,* the show that gives Italy its characteristic social elegance.

As is the case with Italy's history, architecture, and cultural personality, a critical sentiment underlying *la bella figura* is that of civility—which is interwoven in both the subtlety and spectacle of Italian daily life. Indeed, Italy's millennium culture has refined the meaning of civility over the centuries, making social interaction one of the most joyful and effortless experiences in Italian life.

The Mindset of Bella Figura

Following the physical and behavioral aspects of *la bella figura* will elevate your sprits and make others want to be around you, but it is also important to cultivate a mental attitude that reflects personal well-being. That includes developing a **positive body image**, a sense of **personal control**, and an **outgoing approach to life**.

Positive Body Image

Italians like who they are, and they like the way they look. They groom their bodies to please themselves and avoid letting social pressures and outside influences dictate to them. That is the key to acquiring a good body image. When we inevitably compare ourselves excessively to others and take media messages to heart, we begin to feel bad about the way we look. The best way to combat these destructive thought patterns is to become aware of them whenever they happen. Keeping a journal will help your memory. When you watch a TV commercial and start criticizing yourself for not having a size-two body like the model in the cola commercial, get your journal out and document the experience. Describe the commercial and how it made you feel. Externalize the negative thoughts in your head by writing them down on paper. Then let reason overpower your emotions by writing out statements that refute those self-effacing thoughts. An example of reason-driven statements might include, "Genetically, it is not realistic for me to strive for to be a size two. I will strive instead to look and feel good whatever my size is." When you practice correcting your self-punishing statements, they will gradually start to taper off and be replaced with supportive thoughts that increase your confidence. A positive body image starts in the mind, and that means we can do something about correcting a negative one.

Psychological research has uncovered a strong positive relationship between well-being and body image. How we feel about our appearance directly affects how we feel about ourselves in general. When we dislike the way we look, we are more likely to feel depressed, anxious, suffer from lowered self-esteem, and spend loads of money on self-improvement gimmicks. An intense disdain of our bodies—called body image disturbance—may even lead to eating disorders, which can be life-threatening. None of us are happy about the way we look 100 percent of the time, but if ordinary self-criticism intensifies, it interferes with our quality of life.

The influence of the mass media is partially responsible for our tendency to berate our looks and make endless attempts to modify them. The frequency with which we compare ourselves to others to see how we "size up" also affects how we feel about our bodies. Society is harder on females in general. The "ideal" female weight as represented by females in the media (actresses, models, etc.) has progressively decreased to that of the thinnest 5 to 10 percent of American women. This means that 90 to 95 percent of us do not measure up to the media's ideal! The results of a longitudinal survey in *Psychology Today* showed that although females who dislike their bodies continue to outnumber men, body dissatisfaction among males has tripled over the last thirty years! Today, even young children are starting to berate their appearances. This is a real concern, since eating disorders typically emerge around puberty and adolescence.

In addition to correcting our self-effacing thoughts, obviously we need to take care of our bodies too, if we want our self-image to be at its peak. Unfortunately, Americans suffer more from body and eating disordered behaviors than any of our Western or non-Western cultural counterparts. Our Mediterranean neighbors might hold the key to a solution. Research shows that one reason Mediterraneans fare so well in fitness is simply that the Spanish, Italians, and French tend to stay away from junk food, rarely eat between meals, and their attitude toward food is not adversarial. As a result, they keep their weight at reasonable levels with minimal effort. Of course, fit bodies boost self-esteem and promote positive self-image!

Italians have apparently also learned how to resist internalizing media messages that put pressure on them to be thin. My own research on body image found that it isn't so much mere exposure to mass media that determines how bad we feel about our appearance, but instead how much we take the message to heart. There is a difference between simply admiring a fashion model's body shape and actually berating ourselves for not having that shape too! Although physical beauty abounds in the *bel paese*, it is important to remember that the concept of *bella figura* has more to do with liking oneself than being born with perfectly symmetrical features. When you accept your limitations and work with what you have, aesthetics become part of the sweet life and not a disturbing obsession to follow the dictates of mass media and their standards of how we should look.

One way to begin turning a negative body image around is to do this simple mirror exercise. Take a good look at yourself in a mirror and verbalize your good features. Everybody has some physical aspects they like about themselves. Play them up. Talk to yourself about them. Is it your eyes, your skin, or your graceful neck? Think about how you can enhance your looks to make you feel good. Subtle touches, like a strategically-placed little gold barrette, some beautiful socks, or clean, polished shoes can do just the trick to lift your spirits and make you feel like a million bucks. In Etruscan times, when a beautiful body was believed to mirror a beautiful soul, pampering yourself was essential. Italy's emphasis on good grooming has continued to coexist peacefully with the anti-vanity teachings of the Catholic Church. As always, the *bel paese* seamlessly integrates contrast and paradox, and certain cultural traits—like *bella figura*—seem to resist extinction. A few extra pounds here or there are not about to send Italians running to the fad diet section of their local bookstore. On the other hand, living a lifestyle that includes eating healthfully, exercising as a part of daily activity, and enjoying caring for one's appearance leaves them in shape and fit for enjoying life serenely.

Personal Control

Being in control of ourselves not only makes us feel more confident, it also makes us more appealing to others. Think about how you feel when you talk to people who are calm and sure of themselves. Before you know it, you start to feel better in their presence. Their demeanor calms you and inspires you. You begin to feel more confident yourself. Salespeople who have these qualities excel, for they make you feel as if they can solve any problem you have if only you had their product.

Interessante!

Parma is a town of colorful artistic tradition, renowned for the famous artists that lived and worked there: from Correggio and Parmigianino to Verdi, Toscanini, Stendhal, and Proust. A sense of artistry and uniqueness is also reflected in its bella figura *fashions. Garments and accessories made in this former duchy are wearable works of art, from the detailed leather belts of G.A. Fashion Belts or Barbieri Cinture, to men's finely tailored trousers and jackets from Equipage and Valdarno, to exquisite women's handbags from Sander's Corradi and Olpan.*

What exactly is personal control and how do we acquire it? Personal control is the belief that what we do about our circumstances *matters*. You will feel empowered and confident when you know and believe you can change most things that happen to you. On the other hand, those who believe that their actions have no effect on their situation usually struggle with feelings of hopelessness and depression. If you don't like your weight, for instance, you can either decide it is your genetic fate to be overweight and give up trying, or you can take action and follow a plan to get into shape. The more definitive action you take, the more you will realize how much of an impact you can make on your own life and on those around you. If you want to gain personal control Italian-style, then start to become an active participant in your own life. Start loving your life by refusing to give in to helplessness. Find ways to make the best of even the worst situations. After all, positive thoughts are a choice we make, and it is just as easy to choose the positive as it is to choose the negative.

You are the architect of your own happiness and of your own life. If you don't like the way it is going, you need only readjust the design. Control your time schedule, for starters. Spending time doing what you enjoy is like putting money in the *bella figura* bank. So get out there and take that language or pottery class you've been wanting to take. Make time for the things you love and sharpen the skills you've been wanting to master. Most important, when you do feel depressed, take out your journal or simply sit in front of the computer and jot down possible actions you can take right now to change your situation. Write everything that comes to mind, no matter how silly it may seem to you at the time. Then choose the most plausible solution and follow through. If it works, great—if not, try out another solution on the list. Inaction—not error—is the enemy of personal control!

Knowing you are able to control what happens to you—even in small ways—will provide you with a greater sense of tranquillity and well-being. Studies have shown that even hospital patients—in settings where most personal control is forfeited—derive a greater sense of physical and psychological well-being when allowed to decide something as small as arranging the plants in their room, choosing what bathrobe to wear, or deciding which activities they would like to do. No one denies that certain things are beyond our control. It is important to be able to identify such situations so that you can interpret them in the most constructive way possible. However, prove to yourself that you can at least control your perspective at times when other elements are beyond your control. In uncertain times, personal control promotes inner peace. If you are a worrier by nature, try writing out your worries in a notebook before going to sleep, then list possible solutions to think about the next day. Handled in this way, problems lose their grip on your serenity.

Researcher Martin Seligman dedicated his life to helping people with depression, which is hallmarked by a sense of helplessness and the perception of loss of personal control. In order to combat emotional helplessness, it is essential to bring irrational or illogical feelings and perceptions back in line with reality. When something negative happens to us, we will often over-dramatize, over-generalize, and think the worst. Perhaps you once had a phone conversation with a friend that ended on a sour note. You may have felt you said something that offended her. Perhaps you even began to wonder if the friendship was starting to deteriorate. Objectively, we can see how silly that is. In reality, this person may have just had a bad day and her mood had nothing to do with you. Italians have mastered the art of not reading too much into things. They will argue with the obvious and leave the tenuous interpretations and subtleties to someone else. Approaching life this way promotes peace of mind and doesn't leave room for grudges and hurt feelings.

We are all prone at one time or another to errors in thinking that don't correspond to what is really happening. Our thoughts and emotions are sometimes irrational and cause us more pain than the unpleasant situation itself. Fortunately, we can learn to be realistic about negative events and refuse to give them the power to take over our emotional well-being by putting our thoughts and emotions into perspective, Italian-style. Italians may complain bitterly about bureaucracy, politics, or who should have won the soccer match, but common irritations and problems don't threaten either their self-esteem or their zest for life. My colleague Analisa believes that Italy's experience of hardship over thousands of years has taught its people how to survive without wallowing in life's disappointments: "I can choose to look back on the past and cry about what I should or shouldn't have done, or become anxious about uncertainties of the future, but all I really have for sure is this moment, and I want to enjoy it. If there are clouds today, I say, well, there may be sun tomorrow. And if there is no sun tomorrow, *pazienza,* patience, I know from experience that eventually it comes out."

An Outgoing Approach to Life

Social isolation is not a commonly-found condition in Italian society. Being around people you care about should be a regular part of everyone's total mental health regime. Good company gives us a sense of camaraderie, alleviates loneliness, and elevates our spirits. Perhaps it is time to take stock of your social life and see where you stand right now. If you are tucked away in a rural area far from most signs of human life, or bogged down with a workweek that barely leaves you time to breathe, start making some changes. Think of ways in which you can enjoy more social interaction. If you plan on watching the Friday night TV movie anyway, why not invite some friends over to watch it with you? If you walk alone for exercise each day, try finding a walking route or biking trail that is densely populated, then look people in the eye as you pass and greet them. Say hello and make small talk when you are waiting in those long supermarket lines. These small changes in the direction of social interaction will make life a little sweeter as it brings you closer to the *bella figura* philosophy that has stood the test of time for an entire culture.

La bella figura is really about celebrating the beauty in all of us—inside and out. It is a philosophy in which thoughts, behavior, and appearance marry to celebrate a type of beauty that transcends age. *La bella figura* is as much about the middle-aged mother running errands in a chic blazer and jeans as it is the young ingenue with gold hoop earrings sparkling beneath her wind-blown hair. It is appreciating the confident older woman in sleek designer eyeglasses who fills the air with the scent of Chanel and the salt-and pepper-haired gentleman who walks like an important film director in his mysteriously opaque shades. *Fare la bella figura*, however, also goes way beyond the clothes, makeup, high-heeled boots, and leather blazers. *Fare la bella figura* sets the prototype for social conduct and personal dignity. It is holding one's head high, standing up straight, and moving with confidence. Making a good impression involves direct eye contact that can range from a welcoming glance to a playful glimmer. *Fare la bella figura* encompasses what American psychologists call emotional intelligence.

Nicola has an art studio deep in the south of Italy. When he isn't showing his work to potential customers or participating in art exhibitions, he sits outside in front of his store—in a shirt and tie—greeting passersby and giving away small sketches to the neighborhood kids. He laughs, chats, shakes hands, and always has a good word for everybody. Nicola makes his corner of the world just a little more *bello*, beautiful, by this living example of the *bella figura* philosophy.

chapter seven

Communicating With
Words or Without

*When negotiating even the smallest deal, Italians must always look
at each other's faces. They read in their opponent's eyes (or catch in
his voice and choice of words) the signs of his stubborn decision or
hidden timidity....Italians were naturally gifted diplomats in the
days when diplomacy was still a responsible and exacting trade.*

—LUIGI BARZINI, *THE ITALIANS*

Italians are age-old masters of the most important quality for success—
good communication skills. You will always have the edge in social and
professional settings if you know how to make your ideas understood
and are willing to listen to the ideas of others. Let's face it, in addition to
being able to do your job well, employers also need to know you will be
able to get along with your coworkers. If you are adept at the fine art of
verbal exchange, you will be comfortable in any situation—from the
stiffest of job competitions to the haughtiest of high-society parties.
On the other hand, inability to express oneself effectively, letting self-
consciousness take over, or coming across as abrasive or offensive can lead
to feelings of isolation and depression. People love to be around those
who have welcoming personalities that put them at ease! Italians are
communicators extraordinaire.

After official work hours, my grandfather Domenico made it a point
to make the acquaintance of everyone in his community. He greeted

everyone with a cheerful *buona sera*, good evening. With the exception of his profound sadness at my grandmother's death, I don't think I ever saw Pop depressed a day in his life. People feel depressed when they feel lonely and disconnected. Domenico had learned to immunize himself against social isolation by using a cheerful smile and a few welcoming words wherever he went. That is all it took! Despite his thick Italian accent, this remarkable immigrant felt confident talking to anyone, no matter their social status. He knew how to put a smile on everyone's face by communicating warmth and acceptance. Pop generally did three things to ease into conversation. He often **made the first move**; he **took time to talk**; and he **made his message positive**.

Making the First Move

When you make the first step to greet another human being, it makes them feel alive and important. Perhaps you, too, have had the experience where a simple smile made your whole day. There are times when we feel lonely and don't have a clue as to how to change our plight. At such times, it is especially important to reach out and convey empathy and solidarity with the human race. Start up a conversation. Let someone into your heart. Don't brush off a "How are you?" with a one-word reply. Delve further. Let a simple greeting open the door to a more extensive interaction. The Italian desire to communicate and form meaningful relationships is a given, and Italians use all tools at their disposal—eyes, hand gestures, vocal intonation, facial expression, and even the whole body, if necessary!—to get their message across.

Italian communication researchers Felice Perussia and Renata Viano say that it is impossible to *not* be communicating. Every behavior communicates something, even silence. It is important to think about what you are really communicating to others. Sometimes a reluctance to reach out when we feel lonely sends the message of, "I don't need you, stay away," the opposite of what really needs to be communicated. Then, because others react by staying away, we erroneously conclude that we must be undesirable. Making the first move will help you see things in a different way. Most people are as anxious as you are about starting a dialogue, yet would be delighted to welcome your initiation.

Sometimes it is best to just delve right in without deliberating too much. Try not to leave room for hesitancy or self-consciousness. In the rare instance that someone is not receptive to conversation, don't take it personally. Although our culture is more individualistic than Italy's, it is nevertheless possible to increase our level of social interaction if we are open and willing to put a bit of time and effort into building a satisfying social network. Italians seek interaction, they look for it, they delight in it, and they make time for it. Since there is no race to the finish line each day, there is plenty of time to listen and talk. We must make more of a concentrated effort to make time for social life—but the payoffs in well-being are tremendous.

Taking the Time to Talk

The other day at lunch hour, as I walked down Fifth Avenue in Manhattan, I had to marvel at the air of elegance. In many ways, it conjured up the *bella figura* you would find in the Italian culture. Everyone blended together beautifully. The mix of clothes, makeup, perfumes, aftershave, and briefcases were all gloriously coordinated. Elegant pedestrians, young and old, male and female, were models of aesthetic perfection. Older ladies in plush beige wore high-heeled linen pumps that matched pearl-adorned dresses. Handsome bankers in gray and navy pinstripes scoured the headlines of the *Wall Street Journal*. Chic young mothers pushed baby strollers at breakneck speeds. Their bobbing babies enjoyed the ride in coordinating hats, shoes, and playsuits. The day was sunny, and a strong breeze helped the rhythm of the race.

If something hadn't been obviously missing from this snapshot—vocal chattering—this scenario would have qualified for the *bella figura* photo album. In Italy, it is almost impossible to get through even *una mezz'oretta*, a half hour, in silence, and any attempt at a fast pace would be endlessly interrupted by extensive greetings and impromptu conversation! In part, this is due to the *non c'e' male* factor, which essentially ensures that a "How are you?" will not be answered in less than ten minutes. *Non c'e' male* means "not bad." An Italian almost never answers "great" when you ask them how they are. It is as if it were culturally unacceptable! Once, two elderly women greeted each other in the center of Parma:

"*Pina, come stai?* How are you?"

"*Eh…non c'e' male.* Not too bad." The woman shrugged her shoulders and shook her head, ensuring an opening for further discussion.

"What's happening?" asked the first woman, taking the cue.

Via Garibaldi was crowded, and the two friends could hardly hear each other from different sides of the streets, with the *motorini* and Vespas racing in an out of the openings between slower automobiles. Pina finally crossed the street to finish telling her story to Concetta, whom she runs into once in a while when she goes into town to window-shop. In the end the two decided to meet the next day at Pina's house day to look at photo albums of each other's families.

"*Allora, a domani.* Until tomorrow!"

"*A domani, ciao.* Until tomorrow, goodbye!"

Italians leave their doors open for neighbors to drop in. They regularly take leisurely strolls down the main street after dinner so they can *fare quattro chiacchere,* shoot the breeze, with friends and acquaintances. Human interconnection is an everyday habit.

Make Your Words Positive

An old Italian proverb says, *"A vorte fa di piu' 'na buona parola di una compagnia di sordati":* Sometimes one kind word is more powerful than an army of soldiers. Although many Italians today are technology enthusiasts, they have yet to let the computer or cell phone replace face-to-face exchange. Words are powerful, and the peace-loving Italian culture prefers the elegance of words to the barbaric throwing of fists. In Italian conversation, you will also note the periodic insertion of silent pauses. The underlying belief is, *"Una bocca chiusa raggruppa nessuno piede,"* if you keep your mouth closed you won't put your foot in it. You can

Interessante!

The people of the Marche section of Italy incorporate a happy blend of northern and southern characteristics, taking neither the emotionality of Naples nor the cool indifference of Milan to the extreme.

Outside of the main tourist spots, most people do not speak English, but will at least try if you offer them the courtesy of learning a few key words and phrases in Italian, such as "Parla inglese?" Do you speak English?

make or break a person's mood with the words you choose to say. Always make sure that your words reflect the goodness of your soul.

The Importance of Dialogue

Some of us, without realizing it, fall into a pattern of ignoring or neglecting our human need to socialize. We have things to do—often so many that we schedule our time from the moment we get up until way after the moment we should be asleep. Once, someone gave me a lovely, leather-bound organizer for my birthday. It came with a one-hour audiocassette of instructions on how to make time for everything you could ever want to do with your day, month, year, and beyond. After listening to the tape and realizing how much of my life would be spent in the daily maintenance of this instrument alone, I decided the last thing I needed was another daily activity eating away at my free time! Instead, with that extra half-hour a day, I could make a phone call to a friend I haven't seen in a while, or invite my next door neighbor in for coffee. That's what I opted for!

Social psychologists believe that no matter what our culture or nationality, we need other human beings for approval, support, friendship, and information. Barbra Streisand's hit song wasn't so far-fetched. People do need people, and most of us are starving for a simple conversation or a chance to be heard. Unfortunately, the art of casual conversation seems to be dwindling. Trains are full of silent commuters these days. People are afraid to make eye contact when walking down the street. Most of us would rather not eat out than invite a stranger to join our table at a restaurant.

It is never too late to find our way back to the simple pleasures of talk and escape the throes of loneliness, depression, and isolation. Connecting with others creates the joy of belonging. Why not dust off the old social skills before we lose them entirely? Even if we never had them, Albert Bandura's research on observational learning confirms that we can learn or relearn social skills—including conversational techniques—simply by watching and imitating people who use them well.

Try clearing some time in your day just to catch up with a friend and simply listen to what they have to tell you. If you're up for improving your communication skills, watch a friend you admire, or watch videos of public figures to whose style you aspire. Join Toastmasters or take a class that will help you get over your shyness and then go on out there and make conversation!

Interessante! Robert Bolton, Ph.D., *believes that people inadvertently reveal how they feel about a relationship through their nonverbal behavior. When a relationship is not going well, a person will stand at a distance, tense their body, and avoid making eye contact.*

Italian society is a hubbub of social skills where even ordinary verbal exchange is elevated to an art form, with no less attention to detail than da Vinci's *Last Supper*. There is color and drama in both speech and gesture. Dialogues frequently come to life as if acting them out on stage. Educators have long known that a flair for the dramatic is what captures the attention of students. The ability to communicate is what joins human souls. Attentive listening is also an important part of the process.

Eminent social psychologist Leon Festinger spent a good deal of his career developing the Social Comparison Theory. According to this theory, we compare ourselves to others in order to figure out where we stand regarding our actions, feelings, and opinions. In order to do this, we need to learn to talk and listen to what others have to say. Carl Rogers, the great humanist psychologist, promoted active listening as a way to convey caring. If you have ever tried talking to someone who looked around the room distractedly as you spoke, you know how that can make you feel. On the other hand, using good eye contact and paraphrasing what the other person is saying, without proffering advice or suggestions, sends a message: "You are important to me." Furthermore, active listening essentially gives others the opportunity to expand, refine, or clarify what they want you to understand about them.

Interpersonal communication is an integral part of the human experience. Daniel Goleman, who introduced a concept called Emotional Intelligence, wrote about the suffering and rejection people often experience when they lack the ability to appropriately express emotion and interact smoothly with others. Being smart about your emotions is every bit as important as any score on an IQ test. If a person comes across as emotionally flat or doesn't understand the implicit rules of communication (e.g., how close to stand, how to regulate vocal tones, how to participate in the rhythm of speech), it will be much harder to get by in our society. In order to connect with others, we need to know how to show appropriate warmth, empathy, assertiveness, self-assuredness, and respect toward friends, family, and coworkers. Some psychologists believe that interpersonal communication is the key to happiness and success in life. Without it, how could we transmit love, joy, anger, or disappointment?

How could we function at work, school, or home? How could we develop and maintain meaningful friendships?

Sigmund Freud believed the hallmark of a healthy personality is the ability to love and work productively. We can't do either if we can't communicate our feelings, thoughts, and ideas. Poor communication is responsible for the dissolution of many marriages and broken families. It is the source of frivolous legal battles. It is one of the causes of adolescent violence at school by kids who were typically judged to be the "quiet types." Often, those quiet types simply lack the ability to express their emotions, so they stuff them in until they explode. Clearly, many of life's satisfactions as well as frustrations hinge on our ability to effect mutual understanding through verbal and nonverbal exchange.

Ways to Communicate alla Bel Paese

Italians don't limit themselves to words when it comes to letting people know what's on their minds. The Italian culture has integrated a variety of modalities into their communication protocol, including **the arts**, **body language**, **joke-telling**, and refining the art of a good old-fashioned **argument**.

The Arts

The history and progression of the arts in Italy reflect the basic need of people to connect with each other and with their history by understanding the messages of great communicators of the past. Italian families go to museums, ballets, theatres, and live operatic performances. Italian children are as captivated by the opera as they are by any number of television shows or films.

Historical emotion flows through the centuries via the classical aria, the Neapolitan love ballad, the ancient mosaic, and the prolific literary passage. Modern-day Italians are as moved by their messages today as their ancestors were when they first conveyed them through their transformation into art. It is impossible to read Petrarca and Boccaccio without being moved by the humanistic perspective on the beauty of nature. It is impossible not to feel Giacomo Leopardi's agonizing cries through the verses of his poetry. A twinge of national pride touches every Italian heart that hears Verdi's operatic message of liberty or Rossini's larger-than-life *Barber of Seville*. One is left breathless by Raphael's *Stanza della Segnatura* where philosophy and theology are simultaneously captured in frescoes. Italians are active spectators of their own history by way of the arts. They can feel what might have been in the hearts of those living during the Holy Roman Empire or those who took part in the First Crusade that led to the capture of Jerusalem. They feel grounded by a framework of history spanning back to before Christ and are profoundly connected to their antiquity as a people. We can do the same by revitalizing the presence of art and literature in our own lives and learning more about the messages passed to us by their creators.

One of Italy's greatest legacies to the world is its contributions to the field of music as a universal vehicle for communication. Music holds an unmistakable place among Italy's repertoire of communication methodologies. Those who create or listen to music understand the power of its message. While unique to each individual, the universal language of music awakens the soul. It makes us feel understood with its capacity to understand our moods. It comforts us. It exhilarates us. From heartfelt Neapolitan ballads to heart-wrenching operatic arias, Italians have revered the power of the musical message for centuries. You can do the same! When you are feeling down and need a pick-me-up—or even if you simply want to set the right mood for your day upon waking—try playing or making some beautiful music and watch how quickly it can change your emotional state. You don't have to know how to play an instrument in order to express yourself through music—you can hum, sing, chant, or beat a drum. Many Americans love to sing in the shower, where we can't be heard! Nonetheless, singing is a beautiful way to express ourselves. Some experts believe that music has a profound influence on your emotional and physical well-being. Music, whether in the form of human voice or musical instrument, is an age-old method of expression that is universally understood.

In many parts of Italy, and especially in the south, you are likely to hear voices uplifted in song, the harmony of a distant concert or chorus, or the celestial lull of a far-away church bell. Music has been an indispensable communication tool since the days of the Roman empire, when it was even declared one of the four major academic disciplines. To the ancient Romans, music signified both moral and civil strength. It was a science that followed the laws of harmony and order. Gregorian chants are still used today to inspire peaceful meditation. The chants, which have their roots in the Italian Christian Church, at one time inspired many Christians who traveled to Rome to hear the works of Saint Gregory. In more recent times, Italian opera sensations like Pavarotti and Bocelli have given foreigners a renewed appreciation and understanding of opera by helping us relate to the lyrics, melodies, and drama in a way we never could before.

In a society that must deal with endless bureaucracy and frequent political corruption, music has always provided a backdrop of calm for the Italian spirit. Professionals today have confirmed the therapeutic benefits of music and have introduced "music therapy" programs into settings as diverse as schools, convalescent homes, hospitals, and prisons. Besides helping with the healing process in mental and physical ailments, music just makes a person feel alive! My Italian grandparents knew nothing about music therapy. They only knew that when they played music on the Victrola, everyone felt like dancing, singing, and being happy. When they did their jobs with songs in their hearts, their dispositions were bright and sunny and everyone liked to be around them.

Music has the power to deliver messages that touch the heart and speak to the emotions. Even for those of us who are "linguistically challenged," music has the power to express what is in our hearts. It has the power to change our moods and move us.

Bring the arts back into your life—grab a friend and visit a museum or art gallery, attend a concert, stroll through a sculpture garden. Talk about how you experience art, and find new ways of expressing yourself by experimenting with your own artistic talent.

Body Talk

We don't always need words to get our points across. Italians convey feelings and ideas—from the obvious to the subtle—with great décor, even without words. A good example is a colleague of mine who headed a large business consortium in the north of Italy. Once, I saw him awe an entire boardroom of foreign clients with his demeanor alone. Even the Raphaelian Madonna on the wall seemed to follow him with her eyes as he entered the room and took his place at the head of the table. Pietro, like most Italians, loved ceremony. About halfway into the business meeting, he jumped to his feet—leaving dignity behind—and raced over to the bookcase, as if either possessed or inspired by the Muse. Thumbing wildly through one of the books, he found the page he was looking for, and raised his voice in song, *all'improviso*, without warning. To the melodies of familiar operatic works, he began to belt out lyrics about prosciutto and reggiano parmesiano cheese. To all of our amazement, the distinguished businessman of a few minutes ago had completely transformed himself into an animated, if not shameless, entertainer. But he had a goal in mind—that of communicating something in an unforgettable way. When at last he finished crooning the final verses of his food-related operetta, his demeanor once again sobered. Then, scrutinizing the astonished faces of those around the table, he flashed a brilliant white smile, remarked in a *bassa voce*, a whisper, "You are all aware that this great city of Parma is renowned throughout the world as the Food Valley, aren't you?" The others looked at each other with relief. This man wasn't all that *pazzo*, crazy. In reality, he was just a master communicator. His foreign colleagues, to this day, have not forgotten his message.

While I don't suggest you need to go quite as far as Pietro in order to bring your interactions to life, emotionally flat communication does convey a message of detachment. If you want to be more interesting and alluring, try aligning your facial expression and body gestures with the messages you wish to get across. Make solid eye contact and use a few gestures where appropriate. Professional speakers know that appropriate posture and gestures are essential for effective communication. If they don't make eye contact with the audience, they can hardly hope to hold their attention. If you feel hopelessly shy, ask a friend to coach you or sign up for a class. Improving your connections to other people will be worth the effort.

The standard facets of communication include **spoken and written language**; **body language**, such as facial expression and gestures; the **people themselves** who are engaged in the interchange; and the **non-spoken rules of exchange**, such as appropriate tone of voice, and the physical distance separating the interlocutors, depending on their level of intimacy. Italian communication style, like everything else in Italy, is a sea of colorful harmony and contrast. It is a blend of all of these particulars into a seamless conveyance of ideas and emotions.

Dante's *Divine Comedy* may have officially made Tuscan the national language, but even today nearly 60 percent of Italians cling to their own dialect, at least when at home and among family members. Because of natural boundaries and terrain textures from *paese* to *paese*, dialect-speaking Italians often can't understand each other through verbal communication alone when they travel to another region. That is part of the reason that gesturing has developed into a viable and vital communication tool.

Everyone knows what certain gestures mean. For example, a nod of the head or a smile communicate universal ideas that people from any culture can understand. Italians from the north or the south can carry out complete conversations using only hand and head movements! Gesturing goes back centuries, but scholars just began documenting its history a little more than one hundred years ago. Neapolitans are credited with being masters of this silent language. There is a gesture for everything; some express even subtle variations of emotion. Anger, for example, can be expressed by biting one's lower lip or clenching a fist, or even through a subtle facial expression. Contrary to television stereotypes of the Italian who is madly flailing his arms and hands about, Luigi Barzini once wrote, "The best [Italian] gestures are often so economical as to be almost imperceptible." Italian children often learn to read subtle facial expression in their parents from a young age. Even a slight drawing together of the eyebrows can read as a warning to a child about to be disciplined. Evidence of gesturing is traceable to ancient Greek and Roman times.

Many of us feel awkward about using our bodies to communicate, or don't know how to use them to appropriately enhance communication. We don't have to use our bodies in a dramatic way to add richness to our communications, but even a subtle involvement of our movements and facial expressions lets others know we are interested and involved in the conversation. It sends a message of, "What you're saying interests me. I am open to this conversation." You don't need to exaggerate with gestures when speaking, but posture, facial expression, and even positioning of the head and torso can be important and show a willingness to be involved.

Personal space is also a cultural phenomenon. While Northern Europeans and North Americans prefer a little more room between interlocutors, Italians like to get up close so they can read your eyes, mouth, and facial movements. Of course, we need to follow the protocol of our own cultural comfort levels, but there are times when our body language may be more distant than it needs to be and turn others off. Physical closeness is a sign of trust and affection, and affectionate touching between friends is another way in which Italians add warmth to their interactions. Italians like to talk to you as if they have known you for years, even if you haven't met them before today. This makes people feel special and at ease. In the *bel paese*, people touch each other's arms as they speak, or interlock arms as they walk along the piazza. They read each other's faces and body language. Most Italians can tell what the other is really trying to say and if he means it!

According to Frank Acuff, an international negotiating strategist, there are five communication tips that people in almost any culture will understand. We can all make use of them in our daily lives. First, it is important to **smile**. A smile is a welcoming opener to any social discourse. A smile draws people in and gives them a friendly feeling. Second, it is important to **dress well** when you go out. This doesn't mean you need a fancy, expensive wardrobe, but it does mean that your clothes and accessories are in good taste and give the message that you respect yourself as well as your social encounters. Third, **lean forward** when talking to show interest in what the other person is saying. Fourth, use **open gestures**. An example might be to extend your arms outward as if to invite the other person to talk with you. Finally, **nod your head** occasionally to let the other person know you are listening and understanding what they are saying.

Most of these tips are used instinctively in *bel paese* interactions. Of course, smiling may or may not be appropriate according to the tone one wants to convey, but dressing well is part of *la bella figura*, and every Italian is aware of how important it is to make a good impression. To an Italian, leaning forward invites greater intimacy, and of course gestures and head-nodding add silent richness to an already colorful array of dialects.

Interessante!

Here are some common Italian gestures:

- *Fingers flicked out from under chin says, "I don't give a damn."*
- *Palms up, pointers and middle fingers touching thumbs, shoulders shrugged: "What do you want from me?"*
- *Pointing index and little finger at a person wishes them bad luck.*
- *Hand waving behind head: "That happened way in the past."*
- *Drilling a finger into your cheek: "delicious."*
- *Both index fingers meeting at the tips means "butting heads."*

One way to be a better communicator—in the tradition of the *bel paese*—is to learn to pay attention to facial expressions. Once, my friend Jill went to Florence to meet an Italian colleague, Daniela, to discuss a business project. After observing her for a while, Daniela told Jill frankly, "Your eyes don't match what your mouth is doing. Tell me, what are your reservations?" Jill couldn't believe Daniela had read her mind. But this is hardly magic to Italians, who simply pay close attention. Psychologists have their own ideas about facial expressions. In fact, psychologist J.A. Hall found that the underlying positivity or negativity in verbal messages is often conveyed by the accompanying nonverbal behaviors such as mouth position. Similarly, psychologist Paul Ekman and his colleagues identified distinct facial expressions and that can be recognized in most cultures. They are the expressions that convey anger, disgust, fear, happiness, sadness, and surprise. People from most cultures read these facial expressions in the same way. However, when we aren't paying attention, or when we're thinking only of what we want to say, we often miss these fundamental cues.

Try slowing down a little and really notice the nonverbal cues you're getting. Respond to those and see what happens—people might begin to feel you can read their minds, too!

A Good Joke to Break the Ice

Extroversion is a personality trait that describes people who like to be around others and feel at ease in their social interactions. If nations could have personalities, Italy's would definitely be extroverted. Interestingly, researchers Costa and McCrae found a strong relationship between extroversion and happiness. Extroverts report experiencing a deeper sense of well-being than do introverts (those who like to spend more time alone) because they tend to socialize more and they are also better communicators. Extroverts will usually be the first to get a conversation rolling. Often, this step is the hardest for many of us to take. We may feel self-conscious, shy, or awkward about starting up a conversation from scratch. A common icebreaker used in Italy is the *barzelletta,* joke. Italians love jokes and witty stories. They may exchange slightly risqué quips through the email among friends or tell milder versions to new acquaintances they run into on the street because they believe a good laugh is good for the soul.

Of course, not everyone is a joke-teller, but what is important is to make an effort to exchange ideas with those around you, using any means at your disposal. You may want to memorize a joke or two and practice their delivery. Or you may just want to share a funny story that happened to you. Laughter is by far the best icebreaker, and you'll feel more comfortable with people as a result.

Whether it is shared laughter over a joke or a good healthy argument, Italians have a genetic predisposition for the nuances of both verbal and nonverbal communication, perhaps deriving from the great ancient Roman orators, whose speaking style has been captured and documented in mosaics and frescoes. Today, their modern progeny, albeit in a less formal manner, deliver equally eloquent arguments in day-to-day life. Italians pride themselves on knowing how to communicate with anyone, whether they speak their language or not. A Roman policeman, Alessandro, once told me he uses any method he can when foreign tourists come to his station to ask for directions. That includes hand gestures, arm movements, and even a few foreign words he looks up in the dictionary. He has also drawn diagrams and sketches to make himself understood. No shyness here!

"I love the challenge of making myself understood," Alessandro told me. "It is wonderful to see the smile of relief on a person's face when they connect with what you are telling them. For a tourist so far away from home, it means a lot."

The farther south you travel in Italy, the more outwardly dramatic conversations become. Emotions may flare during the course of conversation, and at times it may seem that human discourse is launched more for the sake of drama and display than to get a specific message across. Life is art, life is spectacle, and Italians paint theirs with a rich, colorful lexicon of subtle and dramatic overtones. Sometimes it is not necessary to get to the specific message. What is important is the experience of human understanding, with words or without.

The Healthy Argument
Among close friends, one way to get a point across is the good old-fashioned argument. Once, I observed two elderly gentlemen standing at the counter of the *bar,* café, about to swallow a cup of strong black coffee in one gulp. Of course, it has to be swallowed at just the right moment, preferably when it can add punch to the drama of the point one is making. One gentleman tells the other he thinks the women of today are crazy. He refers to the first female Italian boxer, a Sicilian by the name of Francesca Lupo. Now what does she have to do that for? And Katia Bellillo, going to bat for her in the Parliament like that. Just the other week she belted Alessandra Mussolini on a national talk show to prove her point. *Che disgrazia,* it's a disgrace. Where's the woman of yesterday? The friend says that maybe it's a good thing. Anyway, if the women got to fight it out in the ring they could spare their *mariti,* husbands, at home. The two friends laugh uproariously at the *battuta,* wisecrack, still looking into each other's eyes, trying to gauge where the other is going with this.

Then the conversation takes a heated turn. It goes deeper into politics. The two friends are now raising their voices and using their hands adeptly to punctuate their sentences. Eventually, they find a point that both agree with, and one friend looks the other clearly in the eye, shakes his head subtlety then thrusts his chin out to the forefront.

"Ehhhh."

Interessante!

Three of the most illustrious communicators in Italian history were Boccaccio, Petrarca, and, of course, Dante Alighieri. Each of these wordsmiths dusted off the world of highbrow literature and made it available to the people. As was typical for medieval times, Dante, and to a certain extent Petrarca, wrote illustriously about love and of the conflict between Heaven and Earth. Boccaccio, in his Decameron, *which marked him as the first Italian novelist, focused exclusively on worldly tales and everyday people as he saw them. His tales were for the people and about the people.*

After a few moments, a jovial conversation resumes on another topic. Each friend has expressed his opinion and been heard.

The next time you and a friend clash a little bit, go ahead and let your friend tell you what he really thinks. Friends don't have to agree on everything. Express yourself too, and then let the argument blow away and find a topic that will make you both happy. As long as you both remain respectful and listen to each other, a good argument won't hurt a good friendship.

chapter eight

A Personal Spirituality

*Stai ferma, in silenzio, e ascolta il tuo cuore. Quando poi ti parla,
alzati e va' dove lui ti porta. (Be still in silence and listen to your
heart. When it speaks to you, arise and go where it brings you.)*
—SUSANNA TAMARO, VA' DOVE TI PORTA IL CUORE

The Italian experience of faith is mostly **personal spirituality** that
makes room for the role of **organized religion** and yet keeps an **open
mind regarding the supernatural.** A sense of God is felt deeply in
the heart of almost every Italian. Even the souls of visitors are often
inspired and renewed by Italy's mystical energy. It hit me one Sunday
morning in the ancient Etruscan town of Perugia, where I was a student years ago. As I pushed open the shutters of my third floor bedroom window, the early morning breezes caressed my cheeks and the
moment suddenly came to a standstill with the sweet scent of flowers,
the fresh aroma of baking bread, and the haunting bellow of the *cam-
pana's* distant chimes spreading like waves over the surrounding *paesini,*
towns. The presence of God was undeniable.

Sociologist Alberto Martinelli believes that Italian society has been
influenced by three factors that give it unity and permanence: the
family, the political party, and, of course, the Church. Religion influences politics and many other facets of Italian life—such as cultural
attitudes, norms of conduct, and social integration—through church-

related volunteer and charitable organizations. One of the major political parties in Italy is the Christian Democratic Party, and while Italy has become more secular since the 1960s, the preservation of religious beliefs and traditions are still part of its genetic code. Even Italian law occasionally acquiesces to the morality of the Church. Divorce, for instance, only became legal in the 1970s, though still very few unhappy couples take advantage of it.

Personal Spirituality

Psychologists confirm that religious faith promotes well-being by conveying a sense of acceptance and hope. Furthermore, there is preliminary research linking religious faith to healing and improved health. Some research findings indicate that, while all faiths confer benefits to those who believe, Christian doctrine specifically gives its followers a sense that God accepts them, and thus the reassurance that one's value in the world doesn't depend on material success. This is comparable to what psychologist Carl Rogers called positive regard—feeling accepted and loved despite our defects. A personal sense of God also gives us hope, a psychological trait that is directly linked to emotional and physical well-being. Interestingly, while many Italians do find solace in going to Holy Mass, most don't feel they have to be in church every week or follow Church dogma literally in order to have a personal relationship with God—which is what is most important.

Despite the strong influence of organized religion, the Italian interpretation of God is primarily felt deep within the individual. There is a fundamental sense of the divine guiding all of one's actions, comforting the soul, and instilling hope in the heart.

One very common way that Italians make God personal is to decorate the home—and often the workspace—with religious artifacts. Hanging proudly on the wall behind my grandfather's cobbler's bench, for example, was a picture of a beautiful haloed Jesus with a glowing heart illuminating his chest. It did not seem out of place in a shoe store accented with ceramic saints, scapulars, and rosary beads, which were strung around industrial strength sewing machines and cans of clear shoe polish. To me it was every bit as normal as the statue of the Infant of Prague my mother kept in her window, whose clothes she changed according to what she needed to pray for that day—green for hope, red for joy, gold for special occasions. My grandmother had a string of plum-sized rosary beads around her headboard and strategically placed bottles of holy water on each post of her four-poster bed. I'm not sure if any of these props were more than simply there to serve as tranquil reminders of one's spiritual connection.

Another way that Italians personalize their religion—albeit more prominently in the south—is through identification with the saints. Saints help to make one's relationship with God more tangible since they were once humans. Like you and me, saints suffered very human physical and emotional frailties, which they were eventually able to rise above. Saints serve as heroes to be emulated as well as inspirational figures to aspire to.

In a mere quarter of a century, Pope John Paul II is responsible for canonizing or beatifying nearly 60 percent of the saints or possible saints in the Catholic Church. There is a saint for every wish you might need to pray for: Saint Blaze protects the throat; Saint Mark the

Interessante!

Italians, whether strictly religious or not, regularly observe rituals of religious origin. Every town and village celebrates festivals with religious connections. Italians are usually named after the saint on whose day they were born, and they celebrate their name day— onomastico—*just as they would their birthday: receiving presents and good wishes from friends and family. Towns also have patron saints for whom they hold festivals followed by fireworks.*
The famous Carnevale in Venice is the pre-Lent festival dating back to the eleventh century. Carnevale means "farewell to meat." Shops close on the more important religious holidays in Italy, which are akin to our secular national holidays in which our libraries and post offices are closed. The religious feasts important enough to close the country include:

Saint Joseph's Day—March 19
Corpus Christi—50 days after Easter
St. Peter and St. Paul—June 29
All Saint's Day—November 1
Immaculate Conception—December 8
Santo Stefano—December 26

ears; Saint Agnes the breasts. Saints are seen as spiritual friends as well as the essential link between the common person and God.

When my grandfather and I were staying with relatives in Calabria, we became used to awakening to the aroma of hot cappuccino and the bustling sounds of the entire family as they prepared for their day. It seemed odd that on one particular morning Pop and I awoke to a silent house that was completely empty. There were no traces of life anywhere to be detected—no voices, no shuffling of feet, no clinking of spoons stirring sugar into coffee cups. It was a hot 16 of August, and, perplexed, we decided to head out into the strong morning sun, along the cobblestone streets, to see if there might be a trace of our family anywhere to be found.

"Zia could have just told us she needed a day off from making the coffee," I joked. But the streets outside were as deserted as my aunt's house was on the inside. We walked until we finally heard faint musical sounds in the distance. As we approached the center of the town, the music grew increasingly louder, finally erupting into a thunderous parade.

"Over there!" I signaled to my grandfather. I pointed to a procession coming out of a church, where a small crowd of faithful laity marched alongside clergy with instruments of brass, woodwind, or percussion—in their hands, in their mouths, or strapped across their chests. Non-performing community members served as either encouraging spectators or impromptu chorus performers as they marched toward a statue of San Rocco.

The holy festival of San Rocco is one of many such *feste* celebrated in little *paesini*, towns, throughout Italy. It is a chance for everyday

Italians to express their unabashed devotion to divinely human figures with whom they can identify and by whom they feel protected. People from the entire town stopped what they were doing that day to come out and lay flowers, fruit, or lire in baskets at the feet of the revered statue of their special saint. Among the cluster of musicians in costume, Pop and I were able to discern the faces of all of our relatives! Everyone offered what they could—their talents, their money, their hearts, their souls—to their patron saint.

According to educator and journalist Annarosa Pacini, there is no one easy explanation as to why saints are so important in Italian religious culture, but they do serve as an example of the ability to cultivate a strong faith in God, despite adversity. The patron saint of a town, such as San Rocco, is seen as protecting the community, the job, or a person's health. Pacini believes that saints serve as the link between heaven and earth. They represent people who overcame physical imperfection and suffering, as did the wounded San Rocco, or difficult situations and hardship, as did the charismatic Mother Teresa. Saint adoration brings faith to a more intimate level for many Italians—sometimes transcending into the mystical or quasi-magical. Italians often make claims about seeing blood or tears streaming from the eyes of their saintly icons. At times it can create public havoc, such as the out-of-control traffic jam that resulted from countless pilgrims flocking to see a ceramic mural of Padre Pio, a famous Italian priest once renowned for many miracles. The mural had to be removed because of the commotion caused by hordes of people who came to see the priest's ribs allegedly bleed. Eminent Italian sociologist Franco Ferrarotti takes a more philosophical view of this widespread Italian phenomenon: "Whenever things aren't going right," says the distinguished professor, "there is always a Madonna that starts crying."

While it is true that Italians get inspired by saints and religious artifacts, making your faith a personal experience can involve reading inspirational stories, visiting interesting and inspiring places of worship, practicing yoga, or listening to mystic music. People have many different ways of getting in touch with their sacred sides. Although the best methods for individualizing faith are the ones that work for you, **meditation**, **prayer**, and a **positive outlook** are some of the most powerful tools you can cultivate to deepen your sense of personal spirituality *all'italiana*, the Italian way.

Learn to Meditate

Meditation for most Italians is not necessarily a forty-minute silent trance. It simply means acquiring the ability to let time stand still for a moment and being receptive to the sights, sounds, and smells around them. Moment-to-moment appreciation is key. For a more traditional form of meditation, you can start out by setting aside ten minutes at the beginning or end of each day. Find a quiet place where you can be alone and will not be disturbed. Sit in a comfortable position and take a couple of slow deep breaths. My favorite relaxing breath is the technique Dr. Andrew Weil writes about and often recommends to his patients. With the tongue placed behind the upper teeth, the idea is to inhale through the nose for a count of four; hold for a count of seven, then exhale through the mouth for a count of eight. I find this technique to be very relaxing when done as a prelude to meditation. Then, after a few of these breaths, you may meditate using any method that you like, from visualization to letting go of all thoughts in your head. Some people like to listen to peaceful music, repeat a positive word or affirmation, or simply focus on the rhythm of their own breathing.

Rediscover Prayer

Rediscovering the prayers of your childhood or simply conversing with God in everyday language will renew and strengthen your spiritual side. The repetition of conventional prayer puts you in a meditative state and after a while you will notice a wave of peace and calm taking over. But prayer does not have to be formal in order for you to experience its benefits. Prayer can be as simple as a sacred thought or a short, informal conversation with God—no script needed. Get into the habit of reciting a quick prayer of gratitude when things are going right. Say a prayer of appreciation whenever you realize that you have people who care about you in your life, enough food to eat, or a comfortable bed on which to sleep. Take comfort in praying when you are lonely, sad, or frightened, or when you need to ask for a special favor. Filling up silences with the presence of God helps ease loneliness and isolation.

Cultivate a Positive Outlook

Despite well-placed cynicism and occasional lamenting, Italians by and large let negativity roll off of their backs like ducks do with water. Remember that you were made exactly according to plan, and the beauty of love—or God—is reflected in your soul. Extend that light and beauty to others by being positive and trimming negativity from your life. Don't entertain self-deprecating thoughts, negative people, or situations that depress you. Avoid movies and television shows that make you feel anxious, saddened, or bored. They are a waste of time and sap your spiritual strength.

The Role of Organized Religion

Italians have made God, not necessarily the Roman Catholic Church, the focal point of their spirituality. However, while the role of organized religion seems to be almost subsidiary, it does continue to claim its rightful place in the everyday lives of Italians. It is there to enrich— not to dictate. While 95 to 98 percent of Italians are baptized, only about 25 percent of them strictly follow the teachings of the Catholic religion. Many families attend Mass primarily on holidays or to celebrate the sacraments, such as baptism, confirmation, or marriage, while fewer and fewer attend Holy Mass every Sunday.

The moral influence of the Church, however, still serves as the foundation of thoughts and actions. The Catholic God is just as easily a punishing force as He is a benevolent father. This God-fearing perspective serves as the underpinning for a sort of altruistic morality. Feeling guilty—within reason—is considered a good thing if it keeps us on the right path. While the Church sets the general ground rules, they are eventually subject to minor—or major—mutations as a result of individual interpretation. Rigid dogma has no choice but to be flexible in a land where institutions are regarded with skepticism and as secondary to the primary unit of family. The Church has, after all, made its share of mistakes, and, because of its historical involvement with politics, has rendered itself the fair target of healthy skepticism.

Thus, despite its agreed-upon role as a moral and ethical guide for Italians, there is also an overt distrust of the Church as an institution—especially when its teachings threaten the autonomy of the family. The Church patriarchy may at times even be felt as conflicting with the patriarchal authority of the family. The Church is fallible—God is not. Consequently, the Church's teachings are forced to coexist alongside the sometimes opposing beliefs of Italians themselves. Survey results reported by e-zine Zoomata.com revealed that today's Italians would feel guiltier for not presenting themselves well (*fare la bella figura*), than they would had they committed one of the classic seven mortal sins of the Church's teaching. Seventy-nine percent of Italians, according to this survey, no longer fear the consequences of sins, while 72 percent think pride—not humility—is indispensable. The once to-be-avoided pride and sloth have now become the revered self-esteem and relaxation! Italians don't question the paradox. They are seasoned experts at going with the flow. Italian culture not only permits a coexistence of antiquity and modernity, but indeed appreciates that which makes life spicy, colorful, and worth living.

In an attempt to adapt to the needs and lives of its parishioners, some churches in Italy are trying late-night hours, such as an "open house" church program at San Vito in Milan. This tiny baroque church opens its doors between 10 P.M. and 1 A.M. on Saturday nights so that young people can casually drop in before or after their dates and listen to music, pray, or write down their worries and leave them at the altar in exchange for Bible verses. While some critics say the Church should be limited to Holy Mass, Catholic Church officials in

Italy are trying to modernize—at least in some ways—in order to hold on to their following.

Riccardo, who lives in the north of Italy, recounted the religious practices of his family regarding their involvement with the Church when he was growing up in a rural section outside of the main city.

"While there have always been distinct differences between how those of us in the north express our faith as opposed to those in the south, there are also different customs between city and rural dwellers. I come from a family of farmers who connected religion to the atmospheric conditions that we depended upon so heavily. Religion gave us a vehicle for hope: hope that we would get enough rain for the crops, hope that we would get enough sun, hope that the frost wouldn't come too early and kill the last of the harvest. Sometimes on Sunday mornings, we would go to church by foot. The women and children walked in front, with the men behind them. We didn't do this every

Interessante!

As hard as the Catholic Church in Italy tries to keep up with the times, there are some things it will simply not compromise on—like the virtual confession of sins. The Pontifical Council for Social Communication issued a document stating that the Roman Catholic Church would rule out the possibility of giving confessions over the Internet. "The Internet is a wonderful instrument for evangelization and pastoral service, but it will never be possible to confess online," said Archbishop John P. Foley, the president of the special council.

Sunday, however, because there was always so much work to do on the farm. In the summer there would typically be a procession at night and we would all march, with candles in hand, carrying a large statue of the Madonna or the patron saint of our town. While my parents didn't go to church much, they did send me, and I served as an altar boy. Once a year there was a Mass in memory of all of the deceased in our community, and on special feast days or holy days, we would say the rosary amongst ourselves at home around the dinner table. My father would start out with the Our Father, and the rest of us would recite the Hail Marys.

"Most of my friends and I, who are all now middle-aged, don't go to church every Sunday, but we do manage to go for holidays, and we certainly all pray a lot on our own, especially when things go wrong and we need to ask for help. But I like to pray even when things are going right, and I want to give thanks. When I ride my Vespa to work I recite prayers, it's a good use of time."

Italian journalist Luigi Barzini once observed that both Catholics and non-Catholics experience something meaningful when they make a pilgrimage to the Church's headquarters in Rome. The Catholics go to see their moral and spiritual leader—the most important representative of God here on Earth. They inevitably feel a sense of awe and renewed faith upon entering an inspiring basilica. Legendary shrines and holy landmarks, such as Assisi, where Saint Francis lived, prayed, and set an example to be followed by all men, inspire visitors no matter their religion. Some visitors, out of curiosity, go to Syracuse, Sicily, where a bust of the Virgin is known to have wept at one time, shedding abundant tears, which under examination were determined to be human. Others are drawn to Italy not exactly for its religious inspiration, but simply because it is a place where, according to Barzini, "life is still gloriously pagan, where Christianity has not deeply disturbed the happy traditions of ancient Greece and Rome." This statement captures the characteristic contrasts inherent in the Italian culture as applied to the realm of spirituality, which is an integral part of daily life.

Church also serves as a keeper of tradition through various religious markers that punctuate the Italian life cycle. Holy events such as the sacraments of Baptism, First Holy Communion, Confirmation, Holy Matrimony, and the Last Rites, are more than rote-performed religious rituals—they make up the core of one's very identity, and each event is dignified by the participation of family and friends.

Formal religion and membership in religious organizations can play an important role in serving as the missing link for those of us who feel the need to belong. Ultimately, Italians take the middle road when it comes to making room for organized religion in their lives. They make room for the teachings and traditions of the formal Church in their internal moral structure and derive a sense of belonging from their participation. Of course, you don't have to be Catholic in order to derive benefits from organized religion. However, if you once belonged to a place of worship that you haven't been involved with for a while, now may be a good time to explore how you feel about getting involved again. Find ways to let organized religion enrich your life—not control it. For some of us, religious organizations can feel like extended family, while for others, the fit might not be right. Only you can decide.

Another option that may take you on an unforgettable journey is to explore the holy teachings of several different religions in search of a more universal wisdom to guide you. Read a wide variety of spiritual and religious materials. Ask questions. Go to different services. You might enjoy reading the *Bhagavad-Gita*, the *Holy Bible*, the *Prophet*, the *Koran*, the Old Testament, or the *Four Noble Truths* of the Dalai Lama, to name a few. Certain passages will most certainly inspire and uplift you.

Open-mindedness toward the Supernatural

The ever-present *paradosso italiano*, Italian paradox, makes Italy's widespread belief in various supernatural phenomena—despite a national religion that forbids it—hardly surprising. Despite the Church's disapproval, superstitious rituals continue to be carried out—in the subtler ways of the north to the more obvious ways of the south. Often we tend to quickly discount belief in the supernatural as frivolous, but there are experts who now believe that such open-mindedness can have a positive effect on our lives. Author and researcher James Hillman believes it is easy to fall victim to scientific psychology—the same area of study that denounces "pseudo-psychologies" such as astrology. The field of psychology, however, has been rather awkward in dealing with unseen phenomena, such as the soul, and often ends up ignoring their very existence.

Most of us are instinctively curious to know things beyond what our ordinary senses can tell us. Leaving room for the possibility of the invisible not only makes life more interesting but also leads to hope and a greater tendency to be open-minded about other arguments as well. Saints, God, astrology, superstition—and even happiness and love—are all invisible and intangible phenomena. Italians are far from a gullible people, yet they retain a general openness to experience which makes life fresh and alive with new possibilities each day.

Belief in supernatural phenomena is, in varying degrees, commonplace among Italians and Italian-Americans. Children might go to school—as I did—with holy medals pinned on their undershirts to ward away any evil. There might be a neighborhood *comare,* godmother, who in some cases may also have the power to break the spell of the evil eye, or the *malocchio.* My own grandmother and mother would often discuss their dreams—not only in terms of their symbolic interpretations—but also in terms of their numerical meaning, to be put to use in playing a lottery game.

According to Frances M. Malpezzi and William M. Clements, authors of *Italian American Folklore,* belief in the *malocchio,* evil eye, phenomenon, is rooted in the southern Italian peasant worldview of fatalism. It is assumed that good fortune cannot last, and that potential threat abounds. To prosper is to invite envy and become the target of harm by those who might be jealous. A compliment that is given with too much emphasis could very well mean someone is sending you harmful vibrations. In order to diagnose and cure illness brought on by *malocchio,* there is a procedure in which olive oil is dropped into a bowl of water. If the oil disperses, the evil eye is present. To counteract it, the female "curer" pierces the oil with a scissors while reciting a prayer or healing formula.

Of course, in America, where success could conceivably be unlimited, the evil eye no longer has a justification. It eventually died out among successive generations of Italian-Americans. Nevertheless, I, like many other *italo-americani*, Italian-Americans, continue to wear an amulet, whose origins lie in its capability to ward off the evil eye. In reality, these trinkets have come to represent a more generalized symbol of both good luck and Italian heritage. Whatever conclusion one draws about the belief in superstition, at the very least it reminds us of a truth that will always be undeniable—there is more to life than just that which is visible. There is a dimension that is just as real as it is beyond our comprehension. Acknowledgment of this intangible reality may be manifested in religious as well as supernatural beliefs, rituals, and practices.

Modern industrial societies have clearly been partial to the "scientific method"—an empirical procedure of observation, gathering evidence, and performing the resultant analyses. This philosophy often gets translated into the behaviors of an entire culture and its individual members. Sadly, we often stop believing in things we cannot see—for example, miracles. Yet, what is faith itself, if not a conviction that an intangible, invisible dimension really exists? For Italians, the lines of faith and superstition are interwoven.

While Italians believe in and even excel in traditional science, many also believe in astrology. Despite not having withstood scientific scrutiny, astrology and other psychic phenomena have traditionally had a strong foothold in the Italian culture. Astrological predictions, for example, do not have a high rate of actually coming true. Furthermore, to date there has been no statistical correlation between zodiac signs and the personality characteristics of people born under these signs. Nevertheless, the curiosity in one's daily horoscope has been one of the invariants of Italian cultural behavior that has been resistant to extinction. Its practice dates way back to the Mesopotamian culture and is deeply intertwined in Italy's history from the times of the Roman Republic to the beginning of the Roman Empire, when astrology influenced even political decisions. When Augustus became the first Roman Emperor in 27 B.C., he had coins stamped with his zodiac sign on their backs. Throughout Italian history, astrology came and went with the zeitgeist. In certain periods, it influenced politics, public opinion, and even the Church itself. During the Renaissance, there were times when popes based their decisions on the configuration of the heavens.

The official Church position (in contrast to the historic actual practices of its constituents) is that a belief in astrology is dangerous because it limits the freedom of man. Such determinism is directly opposed to the sacred concept of free will, thus enslaving us to the positioning of the stars. Italians themselves don't see it that way. Like the Church, the possibility of unexplainable phenomena has its

Interessante!

Some of the main religious holidays in Italy include:

Epifania: *on January 6,* la befana, *the old woman, carries a bag filled with gifts and toys that she leaves for good children, and coal that she leaves for the bad ones.*

Mercoledi' delle Cenere: *Ash Wednesday, which is when Lent begins for Catholics all over the world*

Domenica delle Palme: *The churches hand out palm leaves as a sign of peace. Churchgoers take palm home and exchange palm leaves with friends and family. They may shape the palm in the form of a cross and leave it on their door, etc.*

Pasqua: Easter Sunday. *This is a time for family gatherings and* la colomba pasquale, *the Easter cake in the shape of a dove, and of course the* uovo di Pasqua, *the chocolate Easter egg wrapped in colored paper.*

place—as a subsidiary dimension that enriches and does not control one's life. The Italian research organization Doxa found that three out of four Italians follow their horoscopes at least occasionally. Those more advanced in years consult their horoscopes to find out about their economic futures and their health, while younger Italians look for information about love and work. And even though Italians are renowned for their skepticism—more so than their American counterparts—there are more horoscope enthusiasts in Italy than there are in the U.S.

In Italy, you can't help but follow the zodiac predictions—in fact, they follow you! Horoscopes are read at regular intervals on radio. They appear in newspapers and countless magazines. Television stations, both national and private, reserve routine airtime for horoscopes. Yet, although Italians consult their horoscopes regularly, most will tell you they don't really believe them but are simply curious as to what they have to say.

Ultimately, extrasensory phenomena, stimuli that cannot be detected through the ordinary senses, are a reminder that we all live with uncertainty. The Italian culture's respect for the supernatural has nurtured a way of coexisting harmoniously with uncertainty instead of coming unraveled when things fail to make sense.

The concept of *la dolce vita* almost defies precise definition, but inherent in its intent is the liberty that comes from not feeling compelled to explain or control everything. *La dolce vita* means trusting yourself enough to go on gut feeling once in a while. It means feeling confident enough to express your intuitive creativity and open yourself up once again to the childlike wonder of fairy tales, magic, miracles, and other phenomena that you cannot see. **Encouraging peak moments** and stopping to **pay attention to your surroundings** are two simple ways you can put wonder back into your own life, even if you have a tendency to lean toward the more tangible and traditional.

Encourage peak moments.

The great humanistic psychologist Abraham Maslow described peak experiences as those moments in which you feel exhilarated and, as a result, come away with a greater enlightenment because of that experience. The actual experience itself can be simple or momentous, but it will always impress you by giving you a greater understanding of the world around you. A momentous occasion such as giving birth or making love would be described as a peak experience for some. Others will suddenly experience a profound change in their understanding when carrying out a common activity like preparing a good meal or taking a walk along the beach. Though you cannot conjure up peak experiences at will, once you figure out when and under what circumstances they occurred, you can try to put yourself in similar circumstances whenever you can.

Stop and look at your surroundings.

Reflecting on your surroundings makes you more open to spiritual experiences. Make contact with nature. Each day, take note of the little things you usually let go by unnoticed. Experience a walk on a mountain trail or through a lush, green field. Notice everything—the sights, the smells, and the sounds. Know what it is like to feel a light rain on your face or taste a snowflake. Remember to appreciate the beauty around you every day, and it will inspire your life in a way that is both tangible and—more profoundly—intangible.

chapter nine

Attitude is
Everything

*From a psychological point of view, if we could import only one
thing from the* bel paese *it would not be designer fashion,
Renaissance art, or gold jewelry from the Ponte Vecchio—the
import that has more potential than anything else to
make us happy is the "made in Italy" mentality.*

The Italian cultural perspective on life is serenely uplifting and colorfully dramatic. It is an attitude that essentially expresses a gourmet
appreciation for every flavor on life's plate. A summary of the secrets
of *la dolce vita* would not be complete without mentioning two of
its most fundamental elements—**a balanced emotional perspective**
and **a savored sense of time**. When put into practice, these two
concepts verify that the key to living a joyously rich life has more to
do with the attitude we practice than it does with external forces like
the situations we face or the possessions we accumulate. Cultivating
a balanced emotional perspective does not mean you have to pre-
tend you are happy about everything that goes on. Italians have no
qualms about making their opinions known loudly and frequently
when things displease them. That is where it ends. All of us face set-
backs, sorrows, and hard times. There is, however, an effective way
to pull ourselves out of emotional slumps by using a few simple

strategies for coping that have long been part of the Italian psychological inheritance.

The *bel paese* **approach to time** is a wise teacher for those of us who at times get pulled into life's chaos and forget how to slow things down. Simple joys, like getting lost in the thrill of a sports game or turning simple gardening into a meditation, help time to stand still momentarily, infusing us with renewed energy.

A Balanced Emotional Perspective

From growing up Italian, I learned there are two basic philosophies for keeping emotions in check: *arrangiarsi* and *accontentarsi*—knowing how to get by and knowing how to make yourself happy with your current situation. If you have ever taken a psychology course, you may have seen the classic reversible figure. Depending how you look at this picture, you can perceive either one light-colored vase against a dark background, or two human silhouettes facing each other against a light background. It is the same picture and nothing has changed. The observer's perspective alone is what changes it from one image to the other. As with the reversible figure, which addresses visual perspective, we also have the capacity to choose our emotional perspective. Happiness is as much a matter of perspective as sadness. Our thoughts have the power to make us feel happy or sad, frightened or anxious.

Antonio, for example, came to this country at the age of nineteen with only a few dollars in his pocket and no formal education or training. He took a job as a waiter, working night shifts, weekends, and anything else he was offered. He lived very frugally so he could put most of his modest paycheck in the bank. Eventually, he married one of the waitresses, an Italian woman who was suffering from Cooley's anemia. Their struggle wasn't easy, but eventually they were able to scrape enough money together to buy a little luncheonette. They started a family. Tony never complained about his plight throughout the years, despite tough times and frequent challenges. When I recently asked him what made him so cheerful, he answered, "Even in rough times, I remind myself that I know how to get by despite what life throws my way. In addition to this, I have good solid work, a wonderful, loving wife, and a beautiful daughter—what more can a man want?" Antonio's perspective—his ability to *arrangiarsi*, get by, and *accontentarsi,* appreciate what he had—was the key to his happiness.

Mi arrangio, I'll get by

The word *arrangiarsi,* according to author Paul Hoffman, means "to make do," or to "make the best of any situation." Italians historically have been acknowledged for their resiliency when it comes to getting out of tight situations: "I'll get by." "I'll make do with what's available to me." "*Pazienza*, patience, if I can't make a purchase because the cashier has no change, I'll get by, I'll wait until later in the day when there's more change in the cash register." "If the vendor tells me there's no more soup in the pot, I'll have the stew." "If we can't afford to eat meat today, we'll make *minestra,* vegetable soup."

Getting by means staying flexible when one road is blocked. You learn to go around it. You find a new road, and learn that that one is just as good. Gina, for instance, wanted to become a surgeon. She loved the idea of healing human illness and pain. When Gina entered the university, she studied hard and followed all premed courses. She scored about average on her medical boards, but when it came time to apply to medical school, she was not accepted. *Mi arrangio*, she said to herself. She was disappointed but not defeated. She spent the next year taking extra science courses and reapplied, only to be rejected the following year as well. Then she decided to find another path, and enrolled in the physician's assistant course at the local university. Because of her premed background, she was able to lop a good deal of time off of the program. She now loves her work, even though it was not her original dream, nor her original path.

We don't have to follow our original dreams to the letter in order to be happy. More important is learning how to be flexible about life and take the side road to happiness when the main road is blocked. Insisting that things go our way at all costs just makes us frustrated and miserable, especially when we are faced with forces that really are beyond our control. Mental inflexibility is contrary to the wise art of *arrangiarsi*. Italians consider resourcefulness to be part of their national identity! In a recent Italian public survey, the majority of respondents said they are proud to be Italian. Many of those respondents also said that what makes them proudest to be Italian is their ability to get by despite chaos or hard times.

M'accontento, being happy with what you have

In addition to being able to roll with the punches, it is also important to learn how to see and appreciate the positive aspects of your present situation. The philosophy of *accontentarsi,* making yourself happy about what you have, is similar, but not identical to that of *arrangiarsi,* the ability to adjust to tough circumstances and find other solutions. *Accontentarsi* eliminates the need to keep up with the Joneses or stockpile possessions that don't make you happy in the long run anyway. Italians are frugal and like to save money more than they like to spend it. On the other hand, they take care of their things and enjoy them for many years. Since inhabitants of the *bel paese* live in close quarters to begin with, fewer things means uncluttered spaces, and uncluttered spaces mean uncomplicated lives. Simplicity is key to *accontentarsi*. It might mean looking in that food pantry and utilizing the canned and boxed goods you already have sitting on the shelves instead of presuming there is nothing to eat and dashing off for fast food. Being happy with what you have means not worrying or feeling embarrassed if you don't have all of the things your friends or neighbors have. Remember, while material possessions can seem like fun in the short run, they are not what make us happy in the long run.

Fortunately, we don't have to be Italian to learn the useful skills of getting by and appreciating the positive aspects of life. There are some simple mental corrections we can learn and apply whenever we feel helpless or blue. For many years, I have taught my clients, students, and readers how to argue with their negative thoughts and apply the mental principle of "rational optimism." This technique can be applied any time your thoughts turn negative. Arguing with your negative thoughts will help turn your perspective from negative to positive in no time at all. Our minds are often barraged with irrational negative thoughts that lead to upsetting emotions. For example, imagine you are standing in a long supermarket line. It is suppertime, and you are hungry and tired after a long day's work. You decide to make a quick stop at the supermarket to pick up one or two things, but instead you find that everyone else had the same idea today. The store is crowded but you finally reach the checkout counter. You wait, look at your watch, and every once in a while glance at the hopelessly slow checkout person. Understandably, all of this is making you cranky! Then suddenly someone shoves you from behind with their metal shopping cart. That does it! You turn around and get ready to let all hell break loose. But what you see is a sweet elderly woman, clinging to her shopping cart for balance. Instantly your ire turns to empathy. What's going on? Very simply, you changed your perspective. In doing so, you felt better too.

The great psychologist Albert Ellis introduced the idea of rational emotive thinking to the world, a simple technique we can all use in a pinch. All you have to do is break your negative emotional states into three components in order to override them. It follows an ABC paradigm, where A is the negative event itself (i.e., the shopping cart jabbing into your back,) B is your belief about the event (some wiseguy is trying to irritate me) and C is the emotional consequence of this belief (I feel angry and upset). Do you see how that cycle works? On the other hand, all you have to do to change that bad feeling (C) is to change your way of looking at the situation (B): "Maybe the person who shoved the shopping cart into my back really couldn't help it, after all." This is what keeping an open, flexible mind is all about. You can use this paradigm when you are faced with tough times as well as when you are just mildly dissatisfied with something. Remember, it is usually your perspective—not the lousy situation itself—that makes a person feel bad. Achieving tranquillity is a matter of simply changing perspectives, just as you would change your visual perspective when looking at the classic reversible figure I mentioned before. If we train ourselves to think differently, we will feel differently—much less miserable! Eventually the process will become automatic.

Savoring Time

Imagine a world where the minutes flow by so effortlessly they almost stand still. Imagine a world in which ancient history blends in with modern technology. Intercultural expert Alfons Trompenaar categorizes Italy's culture as past/present. Cultures oriented in the past/present show respect for ancestors and elders and interpret current events in light of past experiences. Living is equally focused on the here and now and no one waits around for the future in order to get on with life. In Italy, time is approximate, flexible, and forgiving. Time is also fluid, continuous, and symbolic—as in the case of refusal to reset the clock at Bologna's train station, even after countless tourists—who don't have a clue—keep missing their trains because it always reads 10:25 A.M. The clock was stopped at the exact time when a terrorist bomb killed eighty-five people and injured two hundred in 1980. To victims' families, survivors, and the majority of Italians, keeping the clock from going forward has great symbolic value.

There are several ways to keep the present from flying by us unappreciated. First, live consciously. Become aware of everything you do and everything your senses experience. Second, keep a daily journal in which you write a reflection each day to keep continuity in your life. This will also help with that feeling of "how did the week/month/year fly by so fast?" Be present-oriented, but also examine the present in light of your past experiences. This will help you develop wisdom and stay connected to the overall picture. Living for the future is like refusing to accept the time you have now. None of us can be certain of a future, but we can feel sure of the present as well as the past, since we have already lived through it. Keep them both in your consciousness and time will always flow effortlessly for you. Some "old country" ways to relish time in the present include getting caught up in the excitement of **sports**, winding down with the tranquillity of **gardening**, and renewing our minds and bodies through a good **vacation**.

Calcio, soccer

Ah, the magic of soccer—how it brings all of Italy to life! Whereas in the U.S. one of the first questions asked of a new acquaintance might be, "What do you do for a living?" the Italian introductory equivalent is, "What soccer team do you root for?" *Calcio,* a phenomenon of the masses, is more entwined in Italian society than baseball is in the U.S.! Soccer is the one unifier that makes even the Milanese feel a sense of brotherhood with the Sicilians—and that is quite a feat! When playing internationally, everyone becomes one Italian family.

Around 2:30 on Sunday afternoon, silence befalls Italy while its people unite with bated breath to watch the television either at home or at the local *bar,* café, and everyone—young and old, men, women, and children—waits for the results of the game.

Italian soccer is not just a sports game; it is a philosophy and a life experience. There is an explosion of cheers, fireworks, kisses, and hugs and a sense of pride as people turn their attention to the celebration of simple play. This represents the spirit of Italy that so many of us admire from afar. It represents a carefree spirit that benefits both mind and body.

One good soccer game can practically close down all of Italy on a Sunday afternoon. It unites the souls of its people, whether rooting for *la Roma* of Rome, *la Juventus* of Torino, *l' Inter* of Milan, *il Parma* of Parma, or *il Milan* of Milan. The jubilance is what is important, and that comes through loud and clear. Every goal creates an earthquake of yelling and cheering and things can get rowdy in the stadiums. Seventy-five thousand people once went screaming through the streets of Rome filled with the festive spirit, waving the *giallorosso* banners with the team colors of Rome, and shouting *Magica Roma!*, Magical Rome! The energy and excitement were contagious and reflected an enjoyment of the simple pleasures of present time. "To be happy," one of my Roman friends said, "all you need is a piece of good bread, a nice ripe tomato, good company...and a ticket to see the game."

You can bring the excitement, joy, and solidarity of sporting events into your life even if you're not wild about soccer or huge crowds. Take a Saturday afternoon at your local park to attend a little league game, and join the excited parents in cheering from the stands. Before you know it, you may find yourself at the stadium, watching the home team and munching on peanuts and Cracker Jacks. The fun and excitement of sports are contagious and in the thrill of such a context, petty cares just vanish.

Il giardino, the garden
The Italian garden is more than the indispensable tomatoes, basil, parsley, zucchini, and mint. It is more than fig trees that must be wrapped in blankets and buried in the winter, or fragrant grape arbors that transform themselves into luscious red or white wine. From the

moment I was old enough to work in the garden alongside my grandparents, I always had the impression that we were dealing with a lot more than fresh fruits and vegetables. Gardening produced a prayerlike state as we felt the earth in our hands, and smelled its sweet aroma. There is no truer communion with nature than this. Gardening works the body and clears the mind. Even if you live in an apartment, you can start a garden in flower pots on your balcony. The effect, though not quite as intense, is still beneficial. Another option is to become part of a neighborhood community garden, where you can either choose to garden in solitude when you want to reflect or weed in good company when you want to exchange ideas.

Italians respect life's energy as it transitions from plant to body. They grow their own food when possible, and then can it, jar it, or store the excess in some way so as to have it last throughout the winter. In the days of my immigrant grandparents, nothing went to waste. Even flowers were relished—dandelions for soup or salad, chamomile for breakfast tea, and fried or frittered zucchini flowers to accompany our meals.

Mushrooming is another hobby that many Italians enjoy. Cousin Luigi always said there is nothing more relaxing than getting out into the forest just as the sun comes up and finding treasure—bunches of flavorful wild mushrooms. Like gardening, mushrooming is a holistic experience that provides a tranquil moment in time and can be combined with good food, good company, and good cheer. (Of course, be sure you know which mushrooms are edible!)

The concept of enjoying time in the garden goes back at least to the elaborate Italian gardens of the Renaissance, where people went cheerfully strolling through elaborately designed works of herbal and floral art in the summertime. Often they would stop to pray or meditate in the cool monastery garden sanctuary. Someone might be bent over collecting medicinal herbs and putting them into his basket, or perhaps gathering some luscious ripe fruit from the orange tree in the distance. What marvelous festivals must have taken place in those magnificent garden settings, which were really extensions of the architectural design of the villas they adorned! The plantings were symmetrical and geometric. There were sections for flowers, fruit, woods, and ponds for fishing or lazing on a boat with the one you love. In that epoch, Italian gardens were planned with the collaboration of artisans, artists, engineers, architects, and plumbers who created cascading fountains that provided a peaceful ambience to those escaping the heat of the city.

Italians have always believed in maintaining strong ties with nature and the earth. Today, Italy is still one of the strongest agricultural countries in the world and is renowned for its farming skills. Even in the south, where the terrain is mountainous and the climate adverse, there is always a healthy production of olives, figs, tomatoes, and capers. When the Italian immigrants came to America, many were attracted to rural areas. Although they were neither expert in the latest U.S. agricultural technology nor familiar with American soil or climate, they nevertheless quickly gained the recognition and respect of their new countrymen for their geniality, their agricultural instincts, and their tenacity in cultivating the land to its fullest abundance.

Our Italian friends must have instinctually known about the psychological importance of spending time working the soil. Today in the U.S., a new branch of psychology called ecopsychology is gaining popularity. Its scope is to reintegrate a part of the field of psychology that has been missing: the importance of maintaining ties with the earth and its link to good psychological health. My Italian family knew nothing of psychology—not to mention ecopsychology—but when they worked alongside each other in the garden something magical happened nevertheless. They felt truly happy. They cared for their gardens as they did their own young, reciting the proverb *figlie vigne e giardino, guardale da vicino*, children, grapevines, and gardens need to be tended closely.

When planning for your own garden—either indoors or out—do what the Italians do and make it an aesthetic as well as a nutritional endeavor. If you have only a corner of your balcony in which you can place potted herbs, arrange everything as you would a little sanctuary, where you can spend of few minutes each day in meditation. Your garden can produce beautiful flowers in colors that calm your mind and purify your thoughts. It can also give you an opportunity to learn new skills or reconnect with old ones that might have dried up from disuse across generations, like making wine, fruit jelly, or pickled eggplant. At the end of a few hours of hard work in the garden, sit and admire it. Think about the meals you will make with your fresh produce. Relax to the sound of water pouring out of the watering can as the sun goes down. Your body will feel nicely relaxed, and your mind will be serene.

The Art of Vacation

In addition to gardening, Italians stop the hands of time by making vacations a priority. *Ferragosto* is the national vacation period during the month of August, in which the whole country seems to close down for several weeks. Stores close, cities are deserted by the local inhabitants, and everyone makes a grand departure to their summer destinations. Plans don't have to be elaborate as long as a clean break is made from the everyday *tran-tran*, routine. Even the long line of stopped traffic on the highway doesn't fluster the carefree vacationer. Italians come prepared. They simply get out of the car, grab a sandwich they brought with them for the occasion, and strike up a conversation with the person stuck in traffic in front or behind them!

The word "leisure" in English comes from the Latin *licere*, which means "permission." In general, there are two categories of people: those who give themselves permission and those who don't. Italians fall indisputably into the first category. They don't kid around when it comes to vacation as a means to "pull the plug" on stress. This characteristic summertime mass exit to ocean campsites and mountains is referred to as the Italian "exodus."

The field of psychoimmunology emphasizes the reciprocal connection between body and mind. Prolonged stress often leads to physical deterioration because our fight-or-flight hormones don't have a chance to wind down and return to normal. It is important to be able to tune out life's daily stressors, of which we are often unaware. One of the ways to wind down is to take a vacation. A real vacation is a vacation from stress. Going on vacation to work on your laptop or to answer work-related cellular phone calls doesn't count as a mental hiatus!

Every summer, Luciano and his wife Irene take her widowed father with them to a little town in the mountains called Pinzolo, about an hour and a half drive away from their home in Parma. In their freshly washed Volvo, to which they have attached their *roulotte*, camper, they battle the impassible Italian highways that remain at a halt for hours at a time during the "exodus" period. They are no different from other Italian families, who drop everything to leave the city behind in search of cool, relaxing places they can enjoy with their children, parents, in-laws, and cousins. Once settled at their destination, Luciano and Irene take long walks in the woods by day, cooling their feet in the mountain streams or just sitting by a rock to watch the clouds go by. Irene's father prefers to stay back at the camper, where he unfolds a chair and reads the sports section of the newspaper or turns the radio on and falls asleep in the sunshine. Simplicity lends itself to tranquillity. Italian vacations don't require big expenditures. Most families camp and bring their own stock of food, eating out only for special occasions while away. Employers, too, know that *vacanze,* vacations, make for happy, productive workers upon their return.

If you want to vacation *all'italiana*, you don't have to go to Italy; all you have to do is remember to make whatever vacation you take be a real change from your everyday routine. If your life is normally hectic and over-scheduled, then going on a group tour where you must see seven cities in five days may not be the ideal solution. Remember, the goal is to get away not only from your physical surroundings, but from your mental routine as well. The greatest obstacle to well-being is a harried attitude. Consider a vacation that puts you back in touch with nature and tranquillity. Explore places that don't mercilessly empty your wallet and add additional stress. Italians believe that the antidote to stressful living is only a vacation away—but please leave the laptop behind!

One of my goals in writing this book was to make the secrets I have learned about *la dolce vita* available to everyone, Italian or otherwise. It is also my hope that Italians will no longer be stereotyped based on prejudicial inaccuracies. Mafia stories may get good TV ratings, but they are anything but a true summation of what Italy or her people are all about. Growing up Italian was something I never thought twice about, I simply knew nothing else. By the same token, it was a life-long transformational process that I became increasingly appreciative of as I grew older. While the American culture is unique in its own right, it is also quite young and can benefit from observations of more time-tested cultures throughout the world, such as Italy's. As a cross-cultural psychology researcher, I believe in the value of our collective ancestral wisdom. My Italian upbringing prompted me to make observations that turned into the psychological questions I would answer years later through my own research and documentation.

One of the most important things I discovered was that many of the cultural skills that helped Italians survive throughout the centuries were manifested right in my home through the words and behaviors of my own family. The same attitudes and behaviors are present in contemporary Italy. They are the invariant elements that make us associate Italy with *la dolce vita*, the sweet life. They are the philosophies that remain indestructible despite the evolution of its society, modernization, globalization, the European Union, and the soaring advances of technology. Essentially, Italians still do what they have always done best—survive—but with a sense of dignity, pride, and joy. Italian-Americans, for this reason, tenaciously hang on to their ancestral bonds. When they are drawn to make a pilgrimage back to Italy, as they often are, they immediately get a sensation of "coming home." Nothing is unfamiliar, even if they have never been there before. The experience of reconnecting to one's roots is nothing less than spiritual and miraculous.

Italian-Americans, however, are not the only ones enamored with Italy and her way of life. Countless people from non-Italian origin refer to Italy with the same passion as they would a new love. They correctly sense that Italy welcomes all of us to participate in its enchantment, no matter what our ethnicity, religion, or language.

Finding the Wisdom of Your Own Cultural Heritage

Thank you for giving me the opportunity to share with you the principles and wisdom of my ethnic heritage. While the connection between positive psychological health and the life-affirming elements inherent to the Italian culture have always seemed obvious to me, I strongly believe that every culture has its own important tenets of universal wisdom. I urge you to rediscover and preserve them. They are the facets that make the American cultural diamond shine.

In an article I wrote for *Italian America* in March of 2000, I coined the term "Italo-actualization," which bounces off the concept of Abraham Maslow's Self-Actualization Theory in psychology. Self-actualization refers to the gradual progression of evolving into all of the wonderful things you were meant to be. Actualization can be thought of as an internal force that guides us instinctively. We need only listen to our inner voices to be guided by our inherent truths. It is my feeling that knowing and preserving your cultural heritage can help you hear your inner voice more clearly. Once we understand the wisdom of our heritage, we can find ways to apply it to our everyday lives with ease and familiarity. As is the case with all of the major world religions, ethnicities share fundamental commonalities across the board, despite differences between particular layers. I call these commonalities universal truths. They are innately imprinted in our souls but often become buried with successive generations as we let those past voices get softer and eventually barely audible. It is important to bring them back to the forefront of our awareness by making a conscious effort to do so.

Using Maslow's paradigm, I would like to give you some ideas for tapping into your own cultural wisdom and preserving it in your heart and in the hearts of generations to follow. Start with a blank spiral notebook, into which you will record all of the information you come across as you carry out your personal cultural exploration into the past. According Maslow's Need Theory, our needs fall into a kind of pyramid shape, with the most pressing physical needs at the larger bottom, which, once satisfied, lead us to crave the fulfillment of the increasingly more spiritual dimensions of our being. In other words, when the basic needs for physical survival are met, we must work toward getting in touch with our souls, the dimension that separates us from all other species on earth.

Physiology and Cultural Wisdom

First, we are instinctively driven to satisfy our most pressing physiological needs, such as food, water, rest, physical exercise, and attention to our health. It is certainly impossible to think on a spiritual level if we are neglecting our bodies by putting the wrong things into them and letting them get run down. Think back a generation or two and try to recall how your ancestors kept their bodies strong and healthy. Before there were modern conveniences, how did they get around? What kind of physical activity did they do around the house and outside? Chances are, your grandparents and great-grandparents had to work hard like mine did. There were no luxuries like being able to go to the gym or popping an aerobics tape into the VCR. In fact, these things didn't exist back then, so the body got a workout by doing the everyday chores it took to keep the house and garden going.

In addition to exercise, healthy bodies had to be nourished with healthy foods. What are some of the specialty dishes in your cultural background? Try to dig up some old family recipes that you can replicate or modify based on your present-day dietary needs and knowledge about the dangers of animal fats, fried foods, and heavy sauces. You can enjoy the best of both worlds—yesterday and today—by making ethnic eating healthier than ever. This is an activity you can share with members of your immediate and extended families. Throw a cultural cooking party, and reminisce about what it might have been like for your predecessors to gather in the kitchen in the "old days." Try to imagine what their daily eating habits were like—chances are they didn't assault their bodies with endless junk food and sedentary living. Was the kitchen the hubbub of activity for your grandparents as it was for mine? What were your family's mealtime customs? Did they enjoy gathering everyone around the table to talk? Did they have special evenings when they packed up the immediate family and headed over to Auntie's house for a covered-dish supper? Try to recreate the wisdom of your cultural heritage as you let familiar kitchen practices nourish your body and soul.

While various types of physical labor kept bodies strong back in the old days, you can be sure that sleep and rest also factored into the healthy-body equation. How did your ancestors like to relax? Did they enjoy reading? Listening to the radio? What time did they go to bed at night? What were their bedtime rituals? Of course, today's lifestyle probably makes it impossible to duplicate their practices exactly, but when you modify and incorporate the philosophy behind these practices, you will gain a sense of authenticity you could never have imagined.

The Cultural Wisdom of Safety

Once you take care of your body, you must respect it enough to keep it safe. Of course, your ancestors probably dealt with different dangers than we deal with today. Interestingly, many modern-day phobias can be traced to real dangers that our ancestors faced. Many people today, for example, have snake phobias, yet most likely they are not living in an environment in which snakes still pose a threat. There are things that do pose threats to our survival, however, and we need to do what it takes to keep ourselves safe and peaceful. That applies not only to physical safety, like making sure you lock the doors of your car at night, but also to safety-oriented practices that promote peace of mind. Do you remember how your ancestors saved money? My grandmother used to keep a piggy bank hidden under the bureau, in which she saved up pennies and odd change for a rainy day. Making sure your financial needs are met and keeping yourself out of debt will help you sleep better at night. Even if your ancestors never had much money, chances are they knew how to put something aside so they wouldn't have to worry about emergencies.

Rituals or behaviors that we do on a regular basis are comforting and promote psychological safety, or peace of mind. Find out what rituals the family of your past ascribed to. Did they have a certain way of celebrating birthdays, holidays, or even daily routines that they followed? Modify as needed to allow them into your life. This will give a depth of meaning to their existence and to yours as you let their wisdom live on and refine itself across new generations.

Love, Belonging, and Cultural Ties

Once our physiological and safety needs are satisfied, we are ready to focus on establishing intimate relationships and making love a part of everything we do. Dig out the old family albums and study the body language of your previous generations. Were they interlocking arms as they posed for the picture? Did they hold each other close as they sat around the table? Were there always friends and neighbors in the pictures? Take a tip from your cultural ancestry and make the time for loving relationships—they are the real food that feeds the heart and soul. We all need to feel like we belong. In the old days, the neighborhood gave a sense of community. Are there ways you can bring that sense of community back into your neighborhood? What about calling up cousins, aunts, and uncles that you haven't heard from in a while? How about joining a civic group that reflects your own ethnic background? I have come across all kinds of ethnic clubs and organizations from Polish-American to African-American. Check them out—participating may very well give you a sense of inner continuity as you reconnect to some old familiar perspectives.

The Cultural Connection to Self-Esteem

Your ancestors, like mine, may have been plain, everyday people, but from their unassuming perspective came a sense of extraordinary pride for doing the best job they could at whatever they did. What kind of work did your ancestors do? Try to find anecdotes about who they were friends with and what their neighbors thought of them. Esteem is important because it relates to how we think of ourselves and how others think of us. You can have the most menial job in the country, but if you do your job the best you can, you develop a sense of self-esteem and dignity that no one can take away from you. You may also have the most important job in the country, but if you approach it with divided attention, you will not gain the respect or esteem of others and eventually you will be unable to feel good about yourself. One way I like to find out more about my cultural heritage, and bolster my self-esteem as well, is to go to the library and find biographies of some of the great figures of my ethnic roots. I study their philosophies and their ways of interacting with others. I find ways in which I can glean something from their ways of conducting themselves that would benefit me in my everyday life. When you reconnect to your roots, you become guided by a desire to make your people proud. It is precisely that spirit that validates and carries on the hard work and contributions that all of our ancestors made toward making America the great country that it is.

Cultural Self-Actualization

Up to this point, we let our cultural underpinnings guide us in satisfying our natural needs of bodily health, safety, love, belonging, and esteem. You'll find that when all of those requirements are satisfied, you will enter a phase where you need something more. You need to develop and deepen your spiritual side. Here, too, turning to the cultural wisdom of your ancestors can help you feel like you've "come home." Think of ways in which your ancestors might have incorporated their spiritual needs into their everyday lives. Were they part of a church group? Did they participate personally in services at the synagogue? Did they read the Bible each night before going to bed? Perhaps organized religion is not right for you. There are other ways your family of the past tended to their spirituality that may be more aligned with your personal philosophy. What about listening to the traditional music of the country that your bloodline came from? What about learning their folklore, or studying the proverbs of your people? Apply what makes sense to your life.

Keep notes on all of the cultural practices of your background. These will serve as a guiding structure along your path to authentic inherited wisdom. Reconnecting to your roots keeps you from having to reinvent the wheel. It is a wonderful, continuous process that will feel right as you get more used to it. In the meantime, my guess is that you will discover that the tenets of my Italian cultural wisdom, while unique in many ways, are also universal in many ways. That is the beauty of learning about other cultures and delighting in each other's differences. What an important lesson to pass on to our children, and to theirs! It is also the secret to turning all of our lives into a *dolce vita* experience.

Dio vi benedica, May God bless you.

references

Chapter 1

Perceptions of Foreign Countries Poll. Gallup Poll, February 2001.

U.S. Dept of State Survey 2000

Margolis, Eric. "Italian Smiles over French Frowns." *Inside Track on World News,* June 3, 2001.

www.tamtamcinema.it

Triandis, Harry C. *Culture and Social Behavior,* New York: McGraw-Hill, Inc., 1994.

www.americanheart.org

Moore, David W. "Only One in Five Americans without a Credit Card," Gallup Poll analysis, May 10, 2001.

Census 2000

www.ISTAT.it/primpag/famiglia.html

Sternberg, Robert. *The triangle of love: Intimacy, passion, commitment.* New York: Basic Books, 1987.

Harms, William. "University of Chicago research shows link between loneliness and health." www-news.uchicago.edu, August 7, 2000.

Silvi, Massimo. *La famiglia italiana? Per Il Censis e' solida, serena, aperta ma ancora tradizionalista.* www.sedicinews.it, 2000

Martinelli, Alberto, Antonio Chiesi, et al. Family Networks and Support Systems in *Recent Social Trends in Italy.* London: McGill Queens University Press, 1986.

Barzini, Luigi. *The Italians.* New York: Atheneum, 1996.

Mautner, Raeleen. "Italo-Actualization: Finding the wisdom of your cultural heritage." *Italian America,* 2000.

Ruth, Sheila. *Issues in Feminism.* Mountain View, CA: Mayfield, 1995.

Seligman, Martin E.P. *Learned Optimism: how to change your mind and your life.* New York: Pocket Books, 1990.

Istat. *Cresce Accesso ad Internet e Uso Cellulare,* it.news.yahoo.com, 2000.

"Mafia Gripping Italian Economy." news.bbc.co.uk/hi/English/world/Europe, Nov 14, 2000.

Chapter 2

"Trompenaar's Cultural Dimensions." shrike.depaul.edu/~jborger/ , Feb 6, 2001.

Kardong, Terrence O.S.B. www.osb.org/gen/topics/work/kard1.html. Assumption Abbey, ND: 1996.

Goleman, Daniel. *Emotional Intelligence.* New York: Bantam, 1995.

Althen, Gary. *American Ways.* Yarmouth, ME: Intercultural Press, Inc., 1988.

Martinelli, Alberto, Antonio Chiesi, et al. *Recent Social Trends in Italy.* London: McGill Queens University Press, 1996.

"Coffee." www.lonelyplanet.com/scoop/eur/ita.htm, July 31, 2000.

Bolton, Robert. *People Skills: How to assert yourself, listen to others, and resolve conflicts.* New York: Simon & Schuster, 1979.

Csikszentmihalyi, Mihaly. *Finding Flow: The psychology of engagement with everyday life*. New York: Basic Books, 1997.

Myers, David G. *The Pursuit of Happiness*. New York: Avon Books, Inc., 1992.

Seligman, Martin E.P. *Learned Optimism*. New York: Pocket Books, 1990.

Lowndes, Leil. *How to be a People Magnet*. Chicago: Contemporary Books, 2001.

Gibran, Kahlil. *The Prophet*. New York: Alfred A. Knopf, 2000.

Chapter 3

Brancatissano, Vincenzo. *Di Bella: l'uomo. La cura. La speranza*. Verona: Positive Press, 1998.

"Trompenaar's Cultural Dimensions." shrike.depaul.edu, 2001.

Prosciutti, Ottavio. *Pagine di Scrittori Italiani*. Perugia: Grafica, 1970.

Sonnet G59. www.pugzine.com/pug4/michelangelo.

Fornari, Carlo. *Maria Luigia: un amore di donna*. Parma: Palatina Editrice, 1997.

Berensen, Bernard. *Italian Painters of the Renaissance*. New York: Meridian World Publishing, 1971.

Plumb, J.H. *The Italian Renaissance: A concise survey of its history and culture*. New York: Harper Torchbooks, 1961.

www.cyberitalian.com/html/gal_11.htm

www.zoomata.com

Hofmann, Paul. *That Fine Italian Hand*. New York: Henry Holt & Co., 1990.

Wilde-Menozzi, Wallis. *Mother Tongue.* New York: North Point Press, 1997.

Tamaro, Susanna. *Va' dove ti porta il cuore.* Milan: Baldini & Castoldi, 1994.

Barzini, Luigi. *The Italians.* New York: Bantam Books, 1964.

Aust, D., and M. Zollo. *Teach Yourself Italian Language, Life, & Culture.* Chicago: NTC Contemporary Publishing, 2000.

Bambino, Richard. *Blood of My Blood.* New York: Anchor Books, 1974.

Sternberg, R.J. "A triangular theory of love." *Psychological Review* 93 (1986), 119-135.

Epstein, Alan. *As the Romans Do.* New York: William Morrow, 2000.

Myers, David G. *The Pursuit of Happiness.* New York: Avon, 1992.

Hillman, James. *The Soul's Code: In search of character and calling.* New York: Warner, 1996.

Ford, Martin E. *Motivating Humans: goals, emotions, and personal agency beliefs.* Thousand Oaks, CA: Sage Publications, Inc., 1992.

Gray, John. *Mars and Venus: starting over.* New York: HarperCollins, 1998.

Lowndes, Leil. *How to Make Anyone Fall in Love with You.* Chicago: Contemporary Books, 1995.

www.ccat.sas.upenn.edu/~haroldsf/popcult/handouts/stereoty/stereotyp.html

Mercuri, Roberta. "Perche piu' lo fai e piu' ne hai voglia."
Panorama, October 2, 2000.

www.tradimento.it

Chapter 4

Epstein, Alan. *As the Romans Do: The delights, dramas, and daily
diversions of life in the Eternal City.* New York: William
Morrow, 2000.

Mautner, Raeleen. "Cross-cultural explanations of body image
disturbance." University of Connecticut: doctoral dissertation,
1998.

Pescosolido, C.A., and Gleason, P. *The Proud Italians: our great
civilizers.* Washington, D.C.: National Italian American
Foundation, 1995.

"Organic food booms in Italy but sales still modest."
www.allhealth.com, June 22, 2001.

"WHO Issues New Healthy Life Expectancy Rankings."
www.who.int/inf-pr-2000/en/pr2000-life.html.

"Vegetarian Fast Food Hits Italy." www.zoomata.com, June 16,
2001.

"Italy by Numbers: Summer Food Festivals." www.zoomata.com,
August 13, 2001.

Martinelli, A., Chiesi, A., and S. Stefanizzi. *Recent Social Trends
in Italy 1960-1995.* Montreal: McGill Queen's University
Press, 1999.

Seifert, K., Hoffnung, R.,and M. Hoffnung. *Lifespan Development (2nd Edition)*. Boston: Houghton Mifflin Company, 2000.

Bell, Brian (Ed.director) *Insight Guides: Italy.* Boston: Houghton Mifflin Company, 1997.

Costantino, M., and L. Gambella. *The Italian Way: aspects of behavior, attitudes, and customs of the Italians.* Chicago: Passport Books, 1996.

Aust, Derek. *Italian language & Culture.* Lincolnwood, IL: NTC Contemporary Publishing, 2002.

Consorzio del Formaggio Parmigiano-Reggiano. *Parmigiano-Reggiano: The only cheese in a class of its own.* Reggio-Emilia, Italy, 2000.

Varona, Verne. *Nature's Cancer-Fighting Foods.* Paramus: Reward Books, 2001.

Chapter 5

Csikszentmihalyi, Mihaly. *Finding Flow: The psychology of engagement with everyday life.* New York: Basic Books, 1997.

"Country Competitiveness Indicators." wbln0018.worldbank.org, 1998.

Orman, Suze. *The 9 Steps to Financial Freedom.* New York: Crown Publishers, Inc., 1997.

deLillo, A., and A. Schizzerotto. *La valutazione sociale delle occupazioni.* Bologna: il Mulino, 1985.

Browne, Joy. *The Nine Fantasies that will Ruin Your Life.* New York: Crown Publishers, 1998.

Gray, John. *How to Get What You Want and Want What You Have.* New York: HarperCollins, 1999.

Myers, David G. *The Pursuit of Happiness: discovering the pathway to fulfillment, well-being, and enduring personal joy.* New York: Avon Books, 1992.

Cacioli, Patrizia. *Acquierello Italiano, anno VIII, #5:* "Come girare il mondo senza una lire in tasca." Nashville: Champs-Elysees, Inc. 1999.

Bach, David. *Smart Women Finish Rich.* New York: Broadway Books, 1999.

Severgnini, Beppe. *Un Italiano in America.* Milan: RCS Libri, 1997.

Althen, Gary. *American Ways.* Yarmouth, ME: Intercultural Press, 1988.

Neighbor, Travis, and Monica Larner. *Living, Studying, and Working in Italy.* New York: Henry Holt and Company, Inc., 1998.

Covey, Stephen R. *First Things First.* New York: Fireside, 1995.

Kenna, Peggy, and Sondra Lacy. *Business Italy: A practical guide to understanding Italian business culture.* Lincolnwood, IL: NTC Contemporary Publishing, 1995.

Aust, Derek. *Italian Language, Life & Culture.* Lincolnwood, IL: NTC Contemporary Publishing, 2000.

Gioseffi, Claudia. *Passport Italy.* San Rafael: World Trade Press, 1997.

Flower, Raymond, and Falassi Alessandro. *Culture Shock! Italy.* Portland: Graphic Arts Center Publishing Company, 1995.

Costantino, Mario, and Lawrence Gambella. *The Italian Way: aspects of behavior, attitudes, and customs of the Italians.* Lincolnwood, IL: NTC Contemporary Publishing, Company, 1996.

Chapter 6

Myers, David G. *The Pursuit of Happiness: discovering the pathway to fulfillment, well-being, and enduring personal joy.* New York: Avon Books, 1992.

Mautner, Raeleen. "Cross-Cultural Explanations of Body Image Disturbance." University of Connecticut: doctoral dissertation, 1998.

National Italian American Foundation. "The Freedom of a Vespa." *Festeggiamo,* Fall 2001.

"Trompenaars' cultural dimensions." shrike.depaul.edu, February 6, 2001.

Lowndes, Leil. *Talking the Winner's Way.* New York: MJF Books, 1999.

Hayman, Gale. *How Do I Look?: The complete guide to inner and outer beauty.* New York: Random House, 1996.

Bandura, Albert. *Social Foundations of Thought and Action.* Englewood Cliffs: Prentice Hall, 1986.

Coon, Dennis. *Essentials of Psycholology: Exploration and Application.* St Paul: West Publishing Company, 1994.

Asselin, Gilles, and Ruth Mastron. *Au Contraire! Figuring Out the French.* Yarmouth, ME: Intercultural Press, Inc., 2001.

Chapter 7

"English as New Latin." www.zoomata.com, May 14, 2001.

"Overview of Happiness Surveys in Italy and U.S." www.eur.nl/fsw/research/happiness/hap_nat/reports, March 17, 2001.

"Marche Voyager, Local Customs." www.lemarche.com/Marche/html/customs.htm, October 7, 2001.

Perussia, Felice, and Viano Renata. *La Comunicazione: aspetti generali.* Milan: Mediserve s.r.l., 2000.

Bolton, Robert. *People Skills: How to assert yourself, listen to others, and resolve conflicts.* New York: Simon & Schuster, 1979.

Bandura, Albert. *Social Foundations of Thought & Action: A social cognitive theory.* Englewood Cliffs: Prentice-Hall, Inc., 1986.

Mautner, Raeleen. "Le note terapeutiche." *America Oggi,* August 12, 2001.

———. "La difesa della lingua." *America Oggi,* June 10, 2001.

Kops, George, and Richard Worth. *Great Speakers Aren't Born: The complete guide to winning presentations.* Hollywood: Lifetime Books, 1997.

Acuff, Frank L. *How to Negotiate Anything with Anyone Anywhere Around the World.* New York: American Management Association, 1997.

Aust, Derek, and Mike Zollo. *Italian Language, Life, and Culture.* Lincolnwood, IL: NTC Contemporary Publishing, 2000.

Coon, Dennis. *Essentials of Psychology: Exploration and Application*. St. Paul: West Publishing Company, 1994.

Chapter 8

Mautner, Raeleen. "La Dolce Vita: Santo Cielo!" *American Oggi*, July 22, 2001.

Myers, David G. *The Pursuit of Happiness: discovering the pathway to fulfillment, well-being, and enduring personal joy.* New York: Avon Books, 1992.

"The Life and Times of Saint Rocco." www.sanrocco.org, July 15, 2001.

Pacini, Annarosa "A cosa servono I Santi?" www.encanta.it/fede_santi.html

www.zoomata.com

"Weeping Statues." www.nhne.com/newsgriefs/nhnenb08.html, March 27, 1995.

www.iltuosito.it/iltuo successo/look.htm

Martinelli, Nicole. "Church opens to Night Crawlers," www.zoomata.com, October 15, 2001.

————. "Holy Chocolate: The Pope Cake," www.zoomata.com, October 15, 2001.

Barzini, Luigi. *The Italians*. New York: Bantam Books, 1972.

Costantino, M., and L. Gambella. *The Italian Way: aspects of behavior, attitudes, and customs of the Italians.* Chicago: Passport Books, 1996.

Aust, Derek. *Italian Language & Culture.* Lincolnwood, IL: NTC Contemporary Publishing, 2002.

Malpezzi, Frances, and William Clements. *Italian-American Folklore*. Little Rock: August House, Inc., 1992.

Althen, Gary. *American Ways*. Yarmouth: Intercultural Press, 1988.

Martinelli, A., Chiesi, A. and S. Stefanizzi. *Recent Social Trends in Italy*. London: McGill Queens University Press, 1999.

Epstein, Alan. *As the Romans Do*. New York: William Morrow, 2000.

"Astrology and horoscopes, chiromancy and cartomancy." www.doxa.it/english/inchieste/oroscopi/intro.html, November 9, 1998.

Hillman, James. *The Soul's Code: In search of character and calling*. New York: Warner Books, 1996.

Carlson, Richard. *Don't Sweat the Small Stuff: and it's all small stuff*. New York: Hyperion, 1997.

Weil, Andrew. *Natural Health, Natural Medicine*. New York: Houghton Mifflin, 1995.

Chapter 9

Mautner, Raeleen. "Quando Freud non serve." *America Oggi,* June 3, 2001.

———. *Change Your Mind, Change Your Weight*. Berkeley, CA: Ronin Press, 2002.

Hoffman, Paul. *That Fine Italian Hand*. New York: Henry Holt & Co., 1990.

"Italy by Numbers: Forgetful Patriotism." www.zoomata.com, October 26, 2001.

Mautner, Raeleen. "La magia del calcio." *America Oggi*, July 1, 2001.

———. "Mammoni? Si, Grazie." *America Oggi*, June 24, 2001.

"Trompenaar's Cultural dimensions." shrike.depaul.edu/~jborger, February 6, 2001.

Ellis, Albert. *A Guide to Rational Living (3rd Rev Ed.)* CA: Wilshire Book Co., 1998.

Pelzer, Dave. *A Child Called "It": One child's courage to survive.* FL: Health Communications, Inc., 1995.

"Telling Time in Bologna." http://www.zoomata.com, October 26, 2001.

Mautner, Raeleen. "L'erba di casa mia." *America Oggi*, August 5, 2001.

———. "Assalto agli stereotipi." *America Oggi*, January 15, 2001.

The Traditional Healthy Mediterranean Diet Pyramid

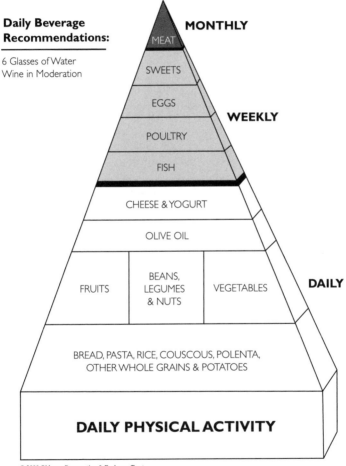

Daily Beverage Recommendations:

6 Glasses of Water
Wine in Moderation

MONTHLY

MEAT

SWEETS

EGGS

WEEKLY

POULTRY

FISH

CHEESE & YOGURT

OLIVE OIL

FRUITS

BEANS, LEGUMES & NUTS

VEGETABLES

DAILY

BREAD, PASTA, RICE, COUSCOUS, POLENTA, OTHER WHOLE GRAINS & POTATOES

DAILY PHYSICAL ACTIVITY

Italian Culture

Aust, Derek. *Italian Language, Life & Culture.* Lincolnwood, IL: NTC Contemporary Publishing, 2002.

Barzini, Luigi. *The Italians.* New York:Atheneum, 1996.

Costantino, Mario, and Lawrence Gambella. *The Italian Way: aspects of behavior, attitudes, and customs of the Italians.* Lincolnwood, IL: NTC Contemporary Publishing Company, 1996.

Flower, Raymond, and Falassi Alessandro.*Culture Shock! Italy.* Portland, Oregon: Graphic Arts Center Publishing Company, 1995.

Hofmann, Paul. *That Fine Italian Hand.* New York: Henry Holt & Co., 1990.

Howard, Edmund. *Italia: The Art of Living Italian Style.* New York: St. Martin's Press, 1996.

Kenna, Peggy, and Sondra Lacy. *Business Italy: A practical guide to understanding Italian business culture.* Lincolnwood, IL: NTC Contemporary Publishing,1995.

Martinelli, A., Chiesi, A. and S. Stefanizzi. *Recent Social Trends in Italy.* Montreal: McGill-Queen's University Press, 1999.

Neighbor, Travis, and Monica Larner. *Living, Studying, and Working in Italy.* New York: Henry Holt & Co., 1998.

Pescosolido, C.A., and P. Gleason. *The Proud Italians: our great civilizers.* Washington: National Italian American Foundation, 1995.

Wright, Nicola. *Getting to Know Italy: And Italian.* Hauppauge, New York: Barron's Educational Series, Incorporated,1993.

Italian History

Burke, Peter. *The Italian Renaissance: Culture and Society in Italy Revised Edition.* Princeton, NJ: Princeton University Press, 1999.

Cole, Trafford R. *Italian Genealogical Records: How to Use Italian Civil, Ecclesiastical, & Other Records in Family Research.* Salt Lake City, UT: Ancestry Publishing, 1995.

D'Epiro, Peter, and Mary Desmond Pinkowish. *Sprezzatura: 50 Ways Italian Genius Shaped the World.* New York: Anchor Books, 2001.

Esposito, Russell R. *The Golden Milestone: Over 2500 Years of Italian Contributions to Civilization (2nd Edition)*. New York: The New York Learning Library, 2002.

Euvino, Gabrielle. *Complete Idiot's Guide to Italian History and Culture*. New York: Alpha Books, 2001.

Hearder, Harry. *Italy: A Short History (2nd edition)*.New York: Cambridge University Press, 2001.

Leland, Charles Godfrey. *Etruscan Roman Remains*. Blaine, WA: Phoenix Publishing, Incorporated, 1999.

Plumb, J. H. *The Italian Renaissance*. Boston: Mariner Books, 2001.

Rosenthal, Margaret F. *The Honest Courtesan: Veronica Franco, Citizen and Writer in 16th-Century Venice*. Chicago: University of Chicago Press, 1992.

Italian Art

Berensen, Bernard. *Italian Painters of the Renaissance*. New York: Meridian World Publishing. 1971.

Bondanella, Peter F. *Italian Cinema: From Neorealism to the Present*. New York: Continuum International Publishing Group, 2001.

Brandon, Anne S. *Artful Italy: The Hidden Treasures*. Montpelier, VT: Invisible Cities Press, 2001.

Marcus, Millicent Joy. *Filmmaking by the Book: Italian Cinema and Literary Adaptation*. Baltimore: Johns Hopkins University Press, 1994.

Paoletti, John T., and Gary M. Radke. *Art in Renaissance Italy*. New York: Harry N. Abrams Inc., 2001.

Turner, Richard. *Renaissance Florence: The Invention of a New Art*. New York: Harry N. Abrams Inc.,1997.

Vasari, Giorgio. *The Lives of the Artists*. Don Mills, ON, Canada: Oxford University Press, 1998.

Wallace, William E. *Michelangelo: The Complete Sculpture, Painting, Architecture*. Southport, CT: Hugh Lauter Levin Associates, 1998.

Italian Cooking

Anthony, Francis. *Cooking With Love, Italian Style*. New York: Hearst Books, 1994.

Casale, Anne. *Lean Italian Cooking*. New York: Random House, Inc., 1994.

D'Amato, Antoinette. *Cooking and Canning with Mama D'Amato*. HarperCollins Publishers, 1997.

Deluise, Dom. *Eat This...It'll Make You Feel Better!: Mamma's Italian Home Cooking and Other Favorites of Family and Friends*. New York: Simon & Schuster, September 1988.

Esposito, Mary Ann. *Ciao Italia Bringing Italy Home: Regional Recipes, Traditions, and Flavors as Seen on the Public Television Series "Ciao Italia"*. New York: St. Martin's Press, 2001.

Medagliani, Eugenio (editor). *Culinaria Italy: Pasta, Pesto, Passion*. Germany: Konemann, 2000.

Palmer, Mary Amabile. *Cucina Di Calabria: Treasured Recipes and Family Traditions from Southern Italy*. London: Faber and Faber, 1997.

Pellegrino, Frank. *Rao's Cookbook: Over 100 Years of Italian Home Cooking*. New York: Random House, 1998.

O'Connell, Marzullo. *365 Easy Italian Recipes*. New York: HarperCollins Publishers, 1991.

Rigante, Elodia. *Italian Immigrant Cooking*. Cobb, CA: First View Books, 1995.

Sidoli, Richard C. *The Cooking of Parma.* New York: Rizzoli International Publications Inc., 1996.

Weil, Andrew, M.D. *Eating Well for Optimum Health.* New York: Alfred A. Knopf., 2000.

Wells, Patricia. *Trattoria.* New York: William Morrow & Company, 1993.

Wright, Jeni. *The Encyclopedia of Italian Cooking.* London, England: Mandarin Publishers, 1981.

Religion and Philosophy

Allegri, Renzo. *Padre Pio A Man of Hope:* Ann Arbor, MI: Servant Publications, 2000.

―――. *The Prophet: Gibran, Kahlil.* New York: Alfred A. Knopf, 2000.

Barish, Eileen. *The Guide to Lodging in Italy's Monasteries.* Scottsdale, AZ: Pet-Friendly Publications, Incorporated, 1999.

Coppa, Frank J. *The Modern Papacy, 1798-1995.* Milano, Italy: Addison-Wesley, 1998.

Englebert, Omer. *Saint Francis of Assisi.* Ann Arbor, MI: Servant Publications, 1990.

Hoare, Rodney. *The Turin Shroud Is Genuine: The Irrefutable Evidence. Updated.* New York: Barnes and Noble, 2000.

Kazantzakis, Nikos. *St. Francis.* New York: Simon & Schuster, 1972.

Korn, Frank J. *A Catholic's Guide to Rome: Discovering the Soul of the Eternal City.* Mahwah, NJ: Paulist Press, 2000.

Lloyd, Susan Caperna. *No Pictures in My Grave: A Spiritual Journey in Sicily.* San Francisco: Mercury House, 1992.

Mayo, Margaret. *Brother Sun, Sister Moon: The Life and Stories of St. Francis.* New York: Little, Brown & Company, 2000.

Norman, Diana. *Siena, Florence, and Padua: Art, Society, and Religion 1280-1400, Vol. 2.* New Haven, CT: Yale University Press, 1995.

Segaard, Matthew (Editor). *Italian Witchcraft: The Old Religion of Southern Europe by Raven Grimassi.* St. Paul, MN: Llewellyn Publications, 2000.

Tomasi di Lampedusa, Giuseppe, et al. *The Leopard: With Two Stories and a Memory (Everyman's Library Series).* Westminster, MD: Everyman's Library, 1991.

Treece, Patricia. *Meet Padre Pio: Beloved Mystic, Miracle Worker, and Spiritual Guide.* Ann Arbor, MI: Servant Publications, 2001.

Italian Literature & Fiction

Alighieri, Dante. *The Divine Comedy: The Inferno, Purgatorio, and Paradiso (Everyman's Library).* New York: Alfred A. Knopf, 1994.

―――. *The Inferno (Wordsworth Classics of World Literature).* Lincolnwood, IL: NTC Contemporary Publishing, 1998.

Binchy, Maeve. *Evening Class.* New York: Bantam Doubleday Dell Publishing Group, 1998.

Caduto, Michael J. and Sarmo, Tom (Illustrator). *The Crimson Elf: Italian Tales of Wisdom.* Golden, CO: Fulcrum Publishing, 2000.

Ciresi, Rita. *Sometimes I Dream in Italian.* Port Huron, MI: Delta, 2001.

DeSalvo, Louise, and Edvige Giunta. (Editors). *The Milk of Almonds: Italian American Women Writers on Food and Culture.* New York: Feminist Press, 2002.

James, Henry. *Italian Hours (Penguin Classics)*, John Auchard (Editor). New York: Penguin USA, 1995.

Labozzetta, Marisa. *Stay With Me, Lella (Prose Series 54)*. Montreal, Canada: Guernica Editions, 1999.

Martin, George (Translator). *Italian Folktales by Italo Calvino*. San Diego, CA: Harvest Books, 1992.

Monardo, Anna. *The Courtyard of Dreams*. New York: Doubleday, 1993.

Neera, et al. *Teresa (European Classics)*. Evanston, IL: Northwestern University Press, 1999.

Papaleo, Joseph. *Italian Stories*. Normal, IL: Dalkey Archive Press, 2002.

Rebay, Luciano (editor). *Introduction to Italian Poetry (A Dual-Language Book)*. New York: Luciano Rebay, 1991.

Rips, Michael. *Pasquale's Nose: Idle Days in an Italian Town*. Newport Beach, CA: Back Bay Books, 2002.

Roberts, Nick (Editor). *Short Stories in Italian (New Penguin Parallel Texts)*. New York: Penguin USA, 2001.

Spencer, Elizabeth. *The Light in the Piazza and Other Italian Tales.* Jackson, MS: University Press of Mississippi, 1996.

Svevo, Italo, et al. *Zeno's Conscience (Everyman's Library).* Westminster, Maryland: Everyman's Library, 2001.

Tabucchi, Antonio, and Frances Frenaye (Translator). *Little Misunderstandings of No Importance.* New York: New Directions, 1987.

Verga, Giovanni. *Cavalleria Rusticana and Other Stories,* G. H. McWilliam (Translator). New York: Penguin USA, 2000.

———. *Sparrow : A Novel by Giovanni Verga, et al.* New York: Italica Press, Inc., 1997.

Italian Language

Aust, D., and M. Zollo. *Teach Yourself Italian Language, Life, & Culture.* Lincolnwood, IL: NTC Contemporary Publishing, 2000.

Burke, David. *The Best of Italian Slang and Idioms.* New York: John Wiley & Sons, 1999.

Dini, Andrea. *Laboratory Manual to Accompany Prego!: An Invitation to Italian, 5th Edition.* New York: McGraw-Hill, 2000.

Lazzarino, Graziana. *Prego: An Invitation to Italian, 5th Edition.* New York: McGraw-Hill, 2000.

Merlonghi, Franca Cella. *Oggi in Italia: A First Course in Italian.* Boston: Houghton Mifflin Company, 1998.

Tomb, Howard. *Wicked Italian for the Traveler.* New York: Workman Publishing Company, Inc., 1988.

Wilde-Menozzi, Wallis. *Mother Tongue.* New York: North Point Press, 1977.

Travel Books—Italy

Bell, Brian (Ed. director) *Insight Guides: Italy.* Boston: Houghton Mifflin, 1997.

Bown, Deni. *DK Eyewitness Travel Guide: Italy (2000 Edition).* New York: DK Publishing, Inc., 1998.

Fodor, Eugene. *Fodor's Naples, Capri, and the Amalfi Coast: The Guide for All Budgets.* New York: Fodor's Travel Publications, Incorporated, 2002.

————. *Fodor's Italy 2002.* New York: Fodor's Travel Publications, Incorporated, 2001.

Gershman, Suzy. *Suzy Gershman's Born to Shop Italy: The Ultimate Guide for People Who Love To Shop.* New York: John Wiley & Sons, Incorporated, 2001.

Gioseffi, Claudia. *Passport Italy.* San Rafael: World Trade Press, 1997.

Kahn, Robert. *City Secrets Florence, Venice, and the Towns of Italy.* New York: Little Bookroom, 2001.

Mayes, Frances. *Bella Tuscany: The Sweet Life in Italy.* New York: Broadway Books, April 2000.

————. *Under the Tuscan Sun: At Home In Italy.* New York: Bantam Doubleday Dell Publishing Group, 1997.

Murphy, Bruce and Alessandra de Rosa. *Italy for Dummies: A travel guide for the rest of us.* New York: Hungry Minds, 2001.

Oelerich, Jeanne. *Rome Walking Guide: Where to Go, Where to Eat, What to Do.* Glencoe, IL: Just Marvelous, 2002.

Simonis, Damien. *Lonely Planet Italy.* Oakland, CA: Lonely Planet Publications, 2002.

Steves, Rick. *Rick Steves' Italy 2002.* Emeryville, CA: Avalon Travel Publishing, 2001.

Italian-American Experience

Bambino, Richard. *Blood of My Blood.* New York: Anchor Books, 1974.

Caroli, Betty Boyd. *Immigrants Who Returned Home.* New York: Chelsea House Publishers, 1990.

Celente, Gerald. *What Zizi Gave Honeyboy: A True Story about Love, Wisdom, and the Soul of America.* New York: William Morrow & Co., 2002.

Epstein, Alan. *As the Romans Do: An American Family's Italian Odyssey.* New York: HarperCollins, 2001.

Ewen, Elizabeth. *Immigrant Women in the Land of Dollars: Life and Culture on the Lower East Side, 1890-1925.* New York: Monthly Review Press, 1990.

Hamill, Pete. *Why Sinatra Matters.* Boston: Little, Brown & Company, 1998.

Krause, Corinne Azen. *Grandmothers, Mothers, and Daughters, Oral Histories of Three Generations of Ethnic American Women.* Boston: Twayne Publishers, 1991.

Malpezzi, Frances M. *Italian-American Folklore: Proverbs, Songs, Games, Folktales, Foodways, Superstitions, Folk Remedies and More.* Little Rock, AR: August House Publishers, Inc., 1998.

Mangione, Jerre, and Ben Morreale. *La Storia: Five Centuries of the Italian American Experience.* New York: HarperCollins, 1992.

Merino, Erica. *Life, Italian Style: Quotes and Quips from Notable Italian Americans.* New York: William Morrow & Co., 1999.

Moramarco, Federico. *Italian Pride: 101 Reasons to Be Proud You're Italian.* New York: Pocket Books, 2002.

Mormino, Gary Ross. *Immigrants on the Hill: Italian-Americans in St. Louis, 1882-1982.* Columbia, MO: University of Missouri Press, 2002.

Panunzio, Constantine M. *The Soul of an Immigrant.* New York: The Macmillan Company, 1922

Parks, Tim. *An Italian Education: The Further Adventures of an Expatriate in Verona.* New York: Avon Books, 1996

Pellegrini, Angelo M. *Americans by Choice.* New York: The Macmillan Company, 1956.

Rolle, Andrew. *The Italian Americans: Troubled Roots*. New York: The Free Press - A Division of Macmillan Publishing Company, 1980.

Talese, Gay. *Unto The Sons*. *New York:* Alfred A. Knopf, Inc., 1992.

Viscardi, Angelino. *West to a Land of Plenty: The Diary of Teresa Angelino Viscardi (Dear America Series)* New York: Scholastic, Inc., 1998.

Wilde-Menozzi, Wallis. *Mother Tongue: An American Life in Italy*. New York: North Point Press, 1997.

Italian Music

Bocelli, Andrea. *Cieli di Toscana*. Universal: October 16, 2001.

Bonvini, Stefano. *Mandolins from Italy*. ARC Music 106732: March 12, 2002.

Bourdon, Rosario, et al. *Caruso Edition, Vol. IV*. Walter B. Rogers and Josef A. Pasternack. Pearl: November 23, 1993.

Frances, Connie. *Italian Collection, Vol. 1*. Polygram Records: November 18, 1997.

Franchi, Sergio. *Romantic Italian Songs*. RCA: November 11, 1997.

Grisman, David. *Traversata: Italian Music in America (Live).* Acoustic Disc: November 6, 2001.

Lanza, Mario. *O Sole Mio: Italian Songs & Arias.* Prism Records 147: August 20, 1997.

Lomax, Alan. *The Italian Treasury: Emilia-Romanga.* Rounder Select: July 3, 2001.

————. *The Italian Treasury: Folk Music & Song of Italy.* Rounder Select: May 18, 1999.

————. *The Italian Treasury: Sicily.* Rounder Select: August 15, 2000.

Montverde, Claudio, et al. *Italian Overtures.* Myung-Whun Chung, et. al. Universal 471566: August 13, 2002.

Pavarotti, Luciano. *The Pavarotti Edition.* Universal 470000: November 13, 2001.

————. *Pavarotti Greatest Hits.* Polygram Records 458000: September 30, 1997.

Peerce, Jan. *Jan Peerce Neapolitan Serenade.* Vanguard Records: June 25, 1994.

Ramazzotti, Eros. *Eros Live (Italian [LIVE])*. RCA International: November 10, 1998.

Rossini, Gioacchino. *Rossini: Overtures*. SO De Montreal/Charles Dutoit. Universal 467427: September 18, 2001.

Various artists. *Cinema Italiano: A New Interpretation of Italian Film Music*. Universal 467050: June 11, 2002.

————. *Eh Paisano! 100% Italian-American Classics*. Rhino Records: January 14, 1997.

————. *Songs of Italian Emigrants (Import)*. Dom Disques: September 8, 1998.

————. *The Most Famous Opera Arias*. Sir Colin Davis, et. al. Capitol 68306: July 19, 1994.

Verdi, Giuseppe, et al. *The Best of Italian Opera*. Tullio Serafin, et. al. Angel Classics 69723: January 21, 1997.

Psychology Books on Happiness

Acuff, Frank L. *How to Negotiate Anything with Anyone Anywhere Around the World*. New York: American Management Association, 1997.

Bach, David. *Smart Women Finish Rich.* New York: Broadway Books, 1999.

Bandura, Albert. *Social Foundations of Thought & Action:A social cognitive theory.* Englewood Cliffs: Prentice-Hall, Inc., 1986.

Bolton, Robert. *People Skills: How to asert yourself, listen to others, and resolve conflicts.* New York: Simon & Schuster, 1979.

Browne, Joy. *The Nine Fantasies that will Ruin Your Life.* New York: Crown Publishers, 1998.

Carlson, Richard. *Don't Sweat the Small Stuff: and it's all small stuff.* New York: Hyperion, 1997.

Conn, Dennis. *Essentials of Psycholology.* St Paul: West Publishing Company, 1994.

Csikszentmihalyi, Mihaly. *Finding Flow: The psychology of engagement with everyday life.* New York: Basic Books, 1997.

Ellis, Albert. *A Guide to Rational Living (3rd Revised Edition).* North Hollywood, CA: Wilshire Book Co., 1998.

Ford, Martin E. *Motivating Humans: goals, emotions, and personal agency beliefs.* Thousand Oaks, CA: Sage Publications, Inc., 1992.

Goleman, Daniel. *Emotional Intillegence.* New York: Bantam, 1995.

Gray, John. *Mars and Venus: starting over.* New York: HarperCollins, 1998.

Hayman, Gale. *How Do I Look?: The complete guide to inner and outer beauty.* New York: Random House, 1996.

Hillman, James. *The Soul's Code: In search of character and calling.* New York: Warner Books, 1996.

Kops, George, and Richard Worth. *Great Speakers aren't Born: The complete guide to winning presentations.* Hollywood: Lifetime Books, 1997.

Lowndes, Leil. *How to be a People Magnet.* Chicago: Contemporary Books, 2001
————. *How to Make Anyone Fall in Love with You.* Chicago: Contemporary Books, 1995.
————. *Talking the Winner's Way.* New York: MJF Books, 1999.

Myers, David G. *The Pursuit of Happiness: discovering the pathway to fulfillment, well-being, and enduring personal joy.* New York: Avon Books, 1992.

Orman, Suze. *The 9 Steps to Financial Freedom*. New York: Crown Publishers, Inc., 1997.

Seligman, Martin E.P. *Authentic Happiness: Using the New Positive Psychology to Realize Your Potential for Lasting Fulfillment*. New York: Free Press, 2002.

——— *Learned Optimism: How to Change Your Mind & Your Life*. New York: Pocket Books, 1998.

Sternberg, Robert. *The triangle of love: Intimacy, passion, commitment*. New York: Basic Books, 1987.

Triandis, Harry C. *Culture and Social Behavior*. New York: McGraw-Hill, Inc., 1994.

Weil, Andrew. *Natural Health, Natural Medicine*. New York: Houghton Mifflin,1995.

www.ansa.it
Italian news. Also has a link for English version.

www.astheromansdo.com
Tours of Rome

www.cyberitalian.com
Learn the Italian language online

www.zoomata.com
Find all of the latest news and stats on the Italy of today.

www.niaf.org
Website of the National Italian American Foundation

www.osia.org
One-stop Italian America (Sons of Italy)

www.italgen.com
Italian Genealogy Homepage. Information that explains the
research process and conditions in Italy.

www.italianwebspace.com
Italian WebSPACE: Italian Web Resources

www.cilea.it/music/entrance.htm
The Italian music homepage.

www.iacelanguage.org
Website for the Italian American Committee on Education

www.italianinfo.net
Italian Info dedicated to Americans of Italian heritage

www.italianamericans.com
Italian interests in America, from genealogy to recipes to learning Italian. Also includes links to organizations and festivals in America that may be of interest to those of Italian descent.

www.italiamia.com
Italian links and products from Italy

www.italian-american.com
Italian-American website of New York. Includes famous Italians.

www.proverbi.it
Italian proverbs from all regions (in Italian)

www.radionostalgia.org
First Italian website for antique radio enthusiasts

www.tuscanyinstitute.com
Writer workshops and villa rentals

www.virtualitalia.com
Resource for enthusiasts of Italian culture

index

A
Alighieri, Dante, 162
Andretti, Mario, 17
Anginette Frosting, 100
As the Romans Do, 79, 101, 121
astrology, 179

B
Bandura, Albert, 147
Barber of Seville, 150
Barzini, Luigi, 1, 9, 141, 174, 175
Bellillo, Katia, 161
Biscotti Glaze, 99
Boccaccio, Giovanni, 150, 162
Bocelli, Andrea, 151
body image, 131-135
body language, 61-62, 128-130, 132, 147, 155
Bolton, Robert, Ph.D., 147

C
Chicago, University of, 1
children: discipline, 7-8; involvement in activities of, 10-11; maturation of, 21
Cicero, Marcus Tullius, 27
Clements, William M., 177
communication skills: and the arts, 149-152; being positive, 145-146; dialogue, 146-149; healthy arguments, 161-162; joking, 159-160; making the first move, 142-143; nonverbal, 154-156, 158
consummate love, 74-75

Coon, Dennis, 132
Correggio, 135
Cortez, Hernando, 93
Costa and McCrae, 159
Csikszentmihalyi, Mihaly, 112

D
da Vinci, Leonardo, 147
Decameron, 162
Doxa, 180

E
Elkind, David, 21
Ellis, Albert, 65, 188
Emotional Intelligence, 148
Epstein, Alan, 79, 101, 121
Eta Meta, 92

F
family: keeping in contact, 13; maintaining traditions, 15, 202-203
Ferrarotti, Franco, 168-169
Festinger, Leon, 148
Foley, John P., 173
forgiveness, 6-10, 47-48
Freud, Sigmund, 149
friendship: cultivating new friendships, 29-30, 36-39; loyalty, 48; tolerance, 46-47

G
gardening, 191-194
Goleman, Daniel, 148

H
Hillman, James, 176
Hoffman, Paul, 185

I
Italian America, 199
Italian American Folklore, 177
Italian Censis, 10, 25
Italians, The, 1, 141
Italo-actualization, 199

J
John Paul II, Pope, 165

K
keeping a journal, 57, 136
Keys, Ancel, 81
kinesics , 128
Kops, George, 155

L
Last Supper, 147
Leopardi, Giacomo, 150
Lupo, Francesca, 161

M
Malpezzi, Frances M., 177
Mamma's Own Biscotti, 99
Marche, 145
marriage: and family, 4-5; common values, 5-6; infidelity, 23; realistic expectations, 2-3
Martinelli, Alberto, 163
Maslow, Abraham, 182, 199, 200
Mediterranean diet, 81-84, 85-88; essential ingredients, 94

Mediterranean Food Pyramid, 81
Meichenbaum, Donald, 9
Mom's Pesto, 98
music therapy, 152
Mussolini, Alessandra, 161

N
Need Theory, 200

P
Pacini, Annarosa, 168
Padre Pio, 168
Parma, 135
Parmigianino, 135
Pavarotti, Luciano, 151
peak experiences, 182
personal control, 135-138
Petrarca, Francesco, 53, 150, 162
physical appearance, 123-127
Pius XI, Pope, 1
Pontifical Council for Social Communication, 173
positive regard, 18, 164
Proust, Marcel, 135
Psychology Today, 133
psychoneuroimmunology, 6

R
Rachele's Anginettes, 100
Raphael, 150
rational emotive thinking, 188
Rogers, Carl, 18, 148, 164
romance: and sensuality, 72-74; and the arts, 69-71
Rossini, Gioacchino, 150

S

scientific method, 178
Self-Actualization Theory, 199
self-arguing, 66
Seligman, Martin, 65, 137
soccer, 190-191
Social Comparison Theory, 148
Spaghetti and Meatballs alla Mamma, 97
Spirituality: holidays, 166, 180; meditation, 169-170; organized religion, 171-173, 174-175; prayer, 170; saints, 165-168; Mother Teresa, 168; Saint Agnes, 167; Saint Blaze, 167; Saint Francis, 174; Saint Mark, 167; Saint Rocco, 167, 168; supernatural phenomena, 176-181
Stanza della Segnatura, 150
Stendhal, Henri, 135
Sternberg, Robert, 74
Streisand, Barbra, 146

T

Tamaro, Susanna, 163
Tomato Sauce, 98
Toscanini, 135
Trompenaar, Alfons, 189

U

U.S. Census, 1

V

Va' Dove ti Porta il Cuore, 163
vacation, 194-196
Verdi, Giuseppe, 135
von Winter, Peter, 24

W

wealth: envy of, 113-115; saving money, 107-110, 111-112; sharing good fortune, 110-111
Weil, Andrew, 169
wine; making, 88-89
working: advantages of, 104-105; as a privilege, 102-103; maximizing productivity, 119-120; minimizing negative aspects, 105-106
Worth, Richard, 155

Z

Zoomata.com, 36, 172, 178

Raeleen D'Agostino Mautner,

assistant professor of psychology at Albertus Magnus College in New Haven, Connecticut, holds a Ph.D. in educational/cognitive psychology. She is a self-help writer, cross-cultural researcher, and international lecturer. In addition to having written articles dealing with the differences between Italian and American culture and a weekly column, *Dolce Vita,* for the Italian language newspaper *America Oggi,* she also founded an Italy–U.S. consultancy. Dr. Mautner is also the author of the self-help book *Change Your Mind, Change Your Weight.* Find more information on Dr. Mautner at her website, www.mindlifesolutions.com.